A Primer on
MONOPOLY AND COMPETITION

A Primer on

The Primer series is under the editorial supervision of
PETER L. BERNSTEIN

Name_____

MONOPOLY
AND
COMPETITION

Willard F. Mueller

 RANDOM HOUSE / New York

For My Mother

Introduction

The past five years I have sat through hundreds of days of hearings as Chairman of the Senate Antitrust and Monopoly Subcommittee. Often as I listened to complex testimony, I expressed the perhaps wistful hope that, somehow or other, more simplification was possible.

Certainly simplification is necessary if we are to deal effectively with our pressing problems, whether they be inflation, collective frustration or the balance of payments. For a common aspect to all of these problems is the impact of monopoly, economic concentration and competition and the degree to which they exist in today's America.

What we are talking about is the price we pay for everything from homes to safety pins; the quality of products and service for everything from TV sets to auto repairs; the frustrations we face in dealing with an impenetrable "establishment." And if, as I believe, a direct correlation exists between economic and political power, we are talking about the very existence and control of our democratic institutions.

But how do we talk intelligently about these problems; how do we effectively solve them unless there is public understanding of the role that antitrust policy—designed to control monopoly and concentration and to insure competition—must play if we are to have any success in dealing with these critical issues. In the past few decades the complexity has made public understanding difficult.

This was not always so. Monopoly, of course, is as old as human greed. Merchants have known for centuries that monopoly means bloated profits and political power. Buyers have known it means high prices and a diminished role in determining one's own destiny. Antitrust developed as a peculiarly American response to such power, in particular, the obvious and flagrant abuses of economic power which occurred in the late 1800's.

It was a simpler world, then, and the abuses were clearly seen and deeply felt. A political movement—the populists—gave unification, purpose and vigor to the fight to keep free enterprise "free."

For years, it was the Populists who were the loudest voices against the economic and social inevitabilities flowing from the concentration of economic power.

But today monopoly and its related effects are more complex and refined; they are more subtle and difficult to discern. They are also more dangerous and far-reaching. Unfortunately as the Populist movement lost its vigor, a void developed and the nation became lethargic and unconcerned about the "new monopoly" and the "new monopolist."

However, in the past few years different—although quieter—voices have been questioning the impact of such concentration on a democratic and free enterprise society. They are alarmed at the rapid momentum responsible for concentration of our national assets in a few hands—a handful answerable only to themselves. They are distressed at venerable liberal statesmen popularizing the view that new technology makes economic concentration inevitable in the face of the clear evidence that it should be taking us down the road to more competition and less concentration.

Dr. Mueller, as this book proves, is one of the most articulate of those new voices. And, he has written a book which provides the necessary simplification without being simplistic. The concepts, the complexities are made understandable without sacrifice of solid and sophisticated analysis. The problems, the abuses, the consequences and some realistic solutions are all here. Certainly it is an important contribution to a full understanding of our most vital national problems.

But its major contribution well may be to assist in developing the constituency needed for a vigorous and imaginative national antitrust enforcement policy.

PHILIP A. HART
United States Senate

Contents

A Primer on
MONOPOLY AND COMPETITION

CHAPTER 1

Fundamental Concepts

For many years competition has occupied a cherished place in United States economic and political history. In its simplest terms, the American economic creed equates competition with economic and political liberty and monopoly with economic and political oligarchy.

What is the origin of this creed? Surely it did not originate in the theories and speculations of economists alone, although these have contributed to it. Most importantly, economic ideas provided a rationale useful in articulating what many believed experience had already taught them.

Adam Smith, professor of moral philosophy at Scotland's Glasgow University, created the first systematic rationale of a competitively organized economy. His great work *The Wealth of Nations* was an extraordinary blending of economic theory, homely observation, and public policy proscriptions, much of it devoted to explaining the superiority of competition over monopoly. Smith was reacting chiefly to government-conferred monopoly, the handmaid of mercantilism, although he also condemned private monopoly.

Smith adopted the French phrase "laissez faire" to convey his theory that the "wealth of nations" will be maximized if every man is free to follow those pursuits which to him seem best. If such freedom is allowed, the resources of the nation would be guided as though by an "invisible hand," and central planning by the state would not be needed to guide the economy. Such reasoning destroyed the central premise of mercantilism.

Smith also distrusted and denounced private monopoly, because it too distorted the economic order and served to clog economic incentive and progress. He thought it inevitable that, left alone, businessmen would pursue monopoly gain at every opportunity. His sentiments on this point are best capsuled in his much-quoted observation that "People of the same trade seldom meet together, even for merriment and diversion, but the conversation ends in a conspiracy against the public, or in some contrivance to raise prices."

John Stuart Mill and the other classical economists sharpened the monopoly concept, increasingly identifying the problem as one flowing from the "fewness" of sellers, not from the avaricious nature of the businessman as such. In the mid-nineteenth century, for example, Mill emphasized that "where competitors are so few, they always agree not to compete. They may run a race of cheapness to ruin a new candidate, but as soon as he has established his footing, they come to terms with him."

The essence of Smith's ideas, then, was that only by abandoning rigid government controls and promoting free economic enterprise could the wealth of nations be multiplied. These ideas fell like rain on seeds already sprouted. By Smith's day, England had already become the workshop of Europe. Richard Arkwright's textile mills employed 5,000 people. The Industrial Revolution was already in motion, and the guild monopolies were disintegrating under the new order. As Wesley C. Mitchell put it, in this environment the strength of Smith's reasoning "kept men fixed on a line of conduct they had rather waveringly been following before, and emboldened them to go farther and farther in the direction which common sense seemed to justify, though the actions ran directly counter to precedent."

It is an interesting coincidence in history that Adam Smith's *The Wealth of Nations* and the Declaration of Independence both appeared in the same year, 1776. The United States Constitution provided a political environment ideally fostering Smith's ideas, especially those urging the throwing off of governmental shackles on business. The founding fathers, greedy for new ideas, were familiar with Smith's concepts. Thus the Federalist papers contain numerous references to the virtues of competition and the sins of monopoly, while Hamilton, in his *Report on Manufactures* (1791), had quoted Smith with firm approval:

> Monopoly, besides, is a great enemy to good management, which can never be universally established but in consequence of that free and universal competition which forces everybody to have recourse to it for the sake of self-defense.

The nineteenth-century American business creed was steeped in the laissez-faire ideas of Adam Smith and even today, nearly 200 years since Smith wrote *The Wealth of Nations,* his basic tenets permeate much talk and thinking about monopoly and competition.

True, Smith's homely illustrations of eighteenth-century monopoly are dated by twentieth-century standards. But it does not necessarily follow that time has made a fiction of the basic principles articulated by Smith.

Consider briefly the role assigned to competition in ordering modern economic activity. Every society must, of course, somehow organize its economic resources, transform them into usable wealth, and distribute this wealth among its populace. Simply put, this procedure requires decisions as to what and how much to produce, how the national output is to be distributed, and how to introduce new products and processes that will increase the future national wealth. How well society performs these tasks determines a nation's material welfare, whether it is a so-called market or free enterprise economy or one organized along wholly different lines.

The American economy relies primarily upon a capitalistic, free enterprise system to perform these tasks. The hallmarks of this system are *free consumption, free enterprise,* and *free labor.*

At the heart of this system is the concept of "consumer sovereignty," the notion that consumers are free agents—free to spend or save; in other words, consumers allocate their income to suit *their own tastes.* Through a multitude of these individual choices, consumers ultimately guide the flow of productive resources. The latter, in turn, are organized largely by private individuals and business concerns, called *private enterprises.* The institution of private property permits an enterprise to own land and other productive resources. The institution of freedom of contract permits it to employ human labor.

A private enterprise elects to engage in those productive pursuits which promise the greatest profit. In making his choice, the manager of the enterprise is guided by the tastes of consumers and his capacity to serve them. Of course—and this is crucial—his ability to serve them will be directly related to his ability to provide them with goods at lower costs than the goods sold by his competitors (who are trying to achieve the same objective).

It should be noted that only when private enterprises are free to behave independently of other enterprises—both private and government—do we have a system of *free enterprise.* Hence, "private enterprise" is not always to be equated with "free enterprise."

Free labor is the other main feature of the American economic system. The worker is free to offer or withhold his services, to organize with other laborers and bargain collectively with employers, to defer employment while acquiring an education, and to leave one job and seek another—all without any direct interference by government or employers. Although labor is a factor of production, American law does not view it as an article of commerce. It is accorded a special status because it is part of the sum of human values in which dignity, well-being, and personal fulfillment are important. The distinction between laborers and enterprisers is not always clear-cut, however, as, for example, in agriculture. And that distinction becomes less clear-cut by the fact that one is free to move from one status to the other.

This is, of course, an overly simplified version of how the American economy is organized. Various government and private actions interfere with or complement the decisions of consumers, enterprisers, and laborers. Moreover, certain important sectors of the economy are not run on the basis of consumer sovereignty—for example, national defense—and others are operated by government—for example, the Post Office Department and the Tennessee Valley Authority. But the great bulk of the American economy is operated by private enterprise and responds to consumer desires, thus requiring the coordination and integration of many decisions by isolated producers and consumers. For the performance of this job, heavy reliance is placed on so-called competitive forces. In theory, the task of coordination and organization is accomplished in a *perfectly competitive* economy. *Perfect competition* means a situation where each buyer and each seller is such a small part of the market that, acting alone, he can have no influence over price or output (hence the term *atomistic* competition). Moreover, buyers and sellers are well informed, and there are no artificial restrictions to the entry of new competitors.

In such a world, sellers would be wholly responsive to prices set by an impersonal market. Each seller would produce those products which promise to bring him the greatest net profit. But since others could enter his trade if profits became abnormally high, the disciplining forces of the market would keep profits around competitive levels, that is, near the level where the enterpriser earned a sufficient return to cover his cost of capital, plus enough more to compensate him for the risks associated with running a business.

Simultaneously, the consumer would allocate his purchases so as to maximize his own satisfaction. Out of these independent decisions of numerous buyers and sellers, the market thus generates signals that ultimately determine which products, and how much of each product, are to be produced and consumed.

The competitive process does more, however, than merely allocate resources among industries. It also decides the fate of particular businesses within each industry. The efficient are rewarded with profits; the inefficient are penalized with losses. An impersonal arbiter dictates that each concern must adopt the most efficient production processes, and provides each with a powerful incentive—the enhancement of profits—to develop better processes and products.

Now suppose that one industry in an otherwise competitive world becomes monopolized. Instead of many sellers, there is only one seller. Because the monopolist has some discretion over prices—he is a price maker, instead of a price taker—he will probably find it possible as well as advantageous to charge higher prices than would have existed if competition had continued. The result will be higher prices and lower output. Consumer sovereignty is thwarted, because too little of the monopolized item will be produced. And not only will consumers suffer from higher prices, but fewer resources—labor and capital—will be employed.

At the same time, the monopolist will not be forced to adopt the most efficient methods of production, simply because no one will challenge him if he does not do so. If leading the complacent life makes him listless, he is unlikely to seek new frontiers to conquer.

Some critics of monopoly go even further, asserting that economic and political freedom are like Siamese twins critically joined—destroy one, and the other will surely die. Henry C. Simons has stated this argument forcibly:

> It seems clear, at all events, that there is an intimate connection between freedom of enterprise and freedom of discussion and that political liberty can survive only within an effectively competitive economic system. Thus, *the great enemy of democracy is monopoly in all of its forms:* gigantic corpora-

tions, trade associations and other agencies for price control, trade unions—or, in general, organization and concentration of power within functional classes.[1]

These, then, are the opposite roles supposedly played by competition and monopoly in a free enterprise economy. The real world, of course, contains few pure monopolies or perfectly competitive industries; rather, most industries contain elements of both competition and monopoly. Most of this primer will deal with the causes, nature, and consequences of various industrial structures between these extreme or limiting cases. But before turning to these matters, let us consider in more detail the basic theory of monopoly.

[1] *Economic Policy for a Free Society* (Chicago: University of Chicago Press, 1948), p. 43.

CHAPTER 2

Theory of Oligopoly

Systematic thought about difficult problems requires abstraction. To attempt the one without the other is to look at everything and to understand nothing. Probing the meaning of monopoly is no exception, and economists concerned with the problem of market power have therefore contrived a number of abstractions concerning the competitive process, abstractions called economic *models*.

A model is not a miniature of reality. Rather, it is like a road map; it points the way without cluttering up the vision with masses of unordered facts. The purpose of a model, then, is to isolate those factors most relevant to the problem being analyzed and to omit irrelevancies and factors of little or only occasional importance.

Economists have been building and rebuilding models of competition and monopoly since Adam Smith's time. Though the classical economists refined Smith's model, they dealt almost exclusively with the polar extremes of perfect competition and monopoly, concepts already touched on in the preceding chapter. The essence of monopoly is control over supply.

By limiting the supply or the quantity of a good placed on the market, the monopolist can set the selling price. He therefore generally aims for the one that maximizes his own profits. Although all businessmen strive to maximize profits, only the seller with some market power can be a price *maker* rather than a price *taker*.

But the single-seller monopoly model, like its opposite, the competitive model, is a sterile abstraction. The real world is made up of neither perfect competition nor perfect monopoly. Instead, it consists mainly of industries containing elements of both competition and monopoly, an in-between condition portrayed in Joan Robinson's and Edward H. Chamberlin's theories of "imperfect" and "monopolistic" competition.[1] These works, appearing simultaneously in 1933, made explicit the existence of a continuum of competitive situations between the polar extremes of competition and monopoly. By identifying and focusing attention on this intermediate ground, they opened up for empirical exploration a vast territory, one that encompasses most existing industrial situations.

SOURCES OF MARKET POWER

Economists have identified three key characteristics of an industry that have a direct bearing on its competitiveness. The character or values of these market attributes play a major role in determining where an industry falls within the competitive spectrum between monopoly and competition. These are:

> The *degree of buyer or seller concentration*, an attribute measured by the number and the size distribution of the selling and buying firms in an industry.
> The *condition of entry* to the industry, a charac-

---

[1] Edward H. Chamberlin, *The Theory of Monopolistic Competition* (Cambridge, Mass.: Harvard University Press, 1933); Joan Robinson, *The Theory of Imperfect Competition* (London: Macmillan, 1933).

teristic measured by the advantage which existing businesses hold in relation to potential new entrants.

The *degree of product differentiation* as among the products of the various sellers in the industry.

These factors, called elements of *industrial* or *market structure,* are key concepts in industrial organization theory, a theory positing that they determine the competitive strategies or *market conduct* of business rivals. In turn, the market conduct of rivals determines the ultimate quality of *performance* in an industry, including size of profits, efficiency of production, rate of progressiveness (as reflected by inventions and innovations), character and variety of product choices given consumers, and size of sales promotion expenditures. The theory of industrial organization is thus deterministic and sequential, on the assumption that causation runs from *market structure* through *conduct,* and ultimately to *performance*.

These, of course, are not the only market factors influencing business performance. As discussed below, the growing conglomeration of business enterprise appears to be another crucial determinant of competitive conduct.

Let us now see exactly how variations in the value of some of these aspects of market structure can influence market conduct and performance.

Market Concentration

A key element of market structure is the number of sellers. As Chamberlin has put it, "A condition of monopoly shades gradually into one of pure competition as the sellers increase in numbers." Why so? Only when sellers are so numerous that each seller has no perceptible share of the market do sellers act entirely independently of one another. Farmers, for example, view one another as neighbors, not as rivals. Each knows that, by itself, the sale of his crop has no perceptible effect on market prices.

The way the number of sellers affects market conduct can best be seen by considering two widely different market situations—one with one hundred sellers of equal size; the other with five sellers of equal size. In the first case, to double his share of the market, a seller would need to take only 1 percent away from each of the other sellers; in the second case, to double his market share, a seller would need to garner 25 percent of the business of each rival. (Economists call the latter type of market structure *oligopolistic,* referring to few sellers, as contrasted to *monopolistic,* referring to single seller, and *atomistic,* referring to numerous sellers.)

In the second case, the five rivals are not likely to ignore one another's business strategies. In a word, they will behave interdependently. When the number of sellers is sufficiently few, they have both the capacity and the incentive to behave the same way a single seller is expected to behave. Hence, in theory, oligopolists may set the same price a monopolist would set. The critical question is, of course, At what level of concentration do oligopolists start to behave as monopolists? Economic theory does not provide a pat answer to this question, leaving it, instead, to empirical investigation. But, as will be seen in Chapter 4, empirical studies have demonstrated the presence of a positive correlation between the level of market concentration and the level of profits. That is to say, other things being the same, as the number of rivals decrease, industry profits increase and draw nearer those found in monopolistic industries.

Condition of Entry

Another key element of market structure is the condition of entry, defined as the amount by which established concerns in an industry can raise prices above competitive levels without attracting new entrants. The height of the "barriers to entry" thus determines just how high prices can be raised before new competitors will be induced to enter the field.

In some respects this element of market structure is even

more basic than the degree of market concentration: the ease
with which new concerns may enter an industry determines, in
the first instance, the degree of market concentration that will
ultimately prevail in an industry. Where barriers to entry are
few, as in farming, there are generally numerous competitors;
where entry barriers are formidable, as in autos, there are only
a few sellers.

But in addition to determining the degree of future concentration, the condition of entry may also play another role in
the competitive process: it may condition the behavior of *existing* firms by placing a limit on the prices they charge. It has
been seen that when seller concentration is high, oligopolists
tend to behave like monopolists. But when oligopolists charge
a high price, it may encourage new competitors to enter the
industry, a probability that may well discourage oligopolists
from charging what the traffic will bear in the short run, lest
doing so induce new entry and thereby eventual erosion of the
high prices—and profits. When oligopolists price to forestall
new entry, they are said to be engaging in "limit pricing,"
which means that *potential* competitors rather than *actual*
ones have set the limit or ceiling on the prices charge. In
other words, whereas market concentration measures the number and the size distribution of existing competitors, the condition of entry measures the competitive impact of potential
competitors. The height of entry barriers determines whether
there are concerns waiting in the wings, ready and able to
enter an industry as prices rise progressively above competitive
levels. Depending on the height of entry barriers, oligopolistic
prices will ultimately fall in the spectrum between competitive
and monopolistic levels.

Joe S. Bain, who has greatly refined the economic theory of
the condition of entry, has identified three main kinds of barriers to entry: (1) absolute cost advantages, (2) product differentiation advantages, and (3) economies of large scale.[2]

Established concerns have an *absolute cost advantage* when

[2] *Barriers to New Competition* (Cambridge, Mass.: Harvard University
Press, 1956).

they have lower production costs at any volume of output than do potential entrants. This advantage may result from the ability of the established concerns to buy their inputs (including borrowed funds) more cheaply than potential entrants, from their preferred access to productive techniques, or from their control of scarce resources. For example, if existing steel companies controlled all iron ore deposits, they could completely foreclose new entry into the steel industry.

When established companies can command higher prices for their products than can new entrants for comparable products, they have achieved a degree of *product differentiation,* a differentiation that often rests on accumulated promotional effort creating strong customer preferences for established brands as opposed to new ones. Familiar examples of products with strong product-differentiation-achieved consumer franchises are Campbell soups and Coca-Cola beverages.

Economies of scale in production and distribution present a barrier to entry when it is required that a new concern, to be efficient, be so large as to represent a sizable portion of the market. Note that the economies-of-scale barrier is not expressed in absolute terms—for example, as the amount of investment required to establish a new company[3]—but rather in terms of the share of industry output represented by an optimum-sized new entrant. This factor is crucial because it determines the amount of business a new entrant must take away from established concerns. The importance of this barrier varies greatly among industries. For example, Bain estimates that, whereas the output of an efficient-sized fresh meat-packing plant is at most 1 percent of industry sales, an efficient tractor manufacturing plant is equal to 10 percent to 15 percent of industry sales.[4]

The values of the above three factors determine the height

[3] This also may be an important entry barrier, one customarily included among the absolute cost barriers, since the new company requiring large funds ordinarily has difficulties getting access to capital at the same interest rate as do established businesses.

[4] Bain, *op. cit.,* p. 78.

of the entry barrier surrounding each industry. They vary not only as among industries but also over time in the same industry. Examples immediately come to mind of industries where the size requirements of efficient units have risen over the past two decades. Perhaps the most dramatic change has occurred in those industries where national TV advertising has become important. On the other hand, when an industry grows larger, it can support an increased number of efficient-sized companies, which is another way of saying that the scale-economy entry barrier has been lowered. The following chapter discusses how these countervailing tendencies are affecting the structure of American industry.

Product Differentiation

The third key structural variable is the *degree of product differentiation*. A seller may convince his potential buyers that his products are significantly different from those of other sellers. Economists label this accomplishment product differentiation.

Such differentiation gives a seller a degree of independence in his pricing and other marketing decisions. In household detergents, for example, the seller of Tide has successfully differentiated his product in the minds of consumers from that of the seller of Rinso. Though the seller of each detergent may well keep a weather eye on the other, the relative prices of the two products may nonetheless vary, within limits, without inducing a massive shift in sales from one to the other. And quite clearly, both the seller of Tide and the seller of Rinso can almost entirely disregard the price and other strategies of a completely unknown brand of detergent. In other words, the stronger the degree of product differentiation, the greater the degree of *pricing independence*. This situation is in contrast to the sale of undifferentiated products (for example, wheat and fresh meat), which depend upon price alone.

In sum, various combinations of the trinity of structural

variables—market concentration, condition of entry, and product differentiation—determine the competitive conduct of sellers. At one extreme, an industry with a few sellers and with completely blockaded entry permits behavior similar to that of monopoly; at the other end of the spectrum, many sellers, easy entry, and identical products (the absence of product differentiation) tend to result in intense competitive rivalry. With few exceptions, most United States industries lie somewhere between these polar extremes. As will be seen in Chapter 4, industrial performance varies accordingly.

But first a final word on the concentration variable of market structure. Students of industrial organization have devoted much effort to measuring the degree, causes, and trends of this phenomenon, partly because more and better data are available about this structural variable than about the others. But, for other reasons, market concentration deserves special attention. First, a change in industrial concentration is the best single measure of changes in the degree of interdependence among oligopolists, and therefore of whether an industry is tending toward monopoly or away from it. Moreover, however, changes in market concentration are generally evidence that changes are occurring in other structural variables less susceptible to direct measurement. This is especially true of changes in the condition of entry. If concentration is declining, barriers to entry are most probably also declining; often the reverse is the case when concentration is on the rise. Thus changes in concentration may serve as a useful proxy of changes in other structural variables, particularly in the condition of entry.

One further preliminary matter should be mentioned here. A frequent criticism of market structure theory is that it is *static* and that it therefore explains only how monopolists or competitors allocate existing resources, rather than predicts the competitive process in a dynamic setting. True, a static model does not explain the dynamic process of industrial change. It does not explain how the new product, the new technology, the new business organization is created and the old one destroyed.

Nonetheless, static models are useful in analyzing real world problems. (Market structure theory shares its static character with all important economic theories, including Keynesian theory.) Perhaps the most important and pervasive characteristic of competitive rivalry is its disciplining influence on business enterprise. When competition threatens profits, the enterprise is *forced* to be alert to new ways of cutting costs, developing new products, and exploring consumers' tastes. There is thus an important distinction between the behavior a monopolist *may* indulge in and that which a competitor is *compelled* to follow.

To be sure, static theories of competition say nothing directly about the process of industrial change, innovation, and growth. Yet these models present important clues on such matters. A monopolist is apt to become moribund when high entry barriers surround his industry and protect him from the competitive gale. In a dynamic setting, the spur of competition is the surest way to cure his malady. A business engages in research and development efforts not for the purpose of discovering ultimate truth but to better its rivals and to gain the lead in the competitive race. In other words, in a competitive, capitalistic economy, business enterprises perform in the public interest because the market compels them to, not because of the benevolence of their owners or managers. The market structure model thus focuses attention on those elements in the market environment that influence the degree of competitive rivalry, even though it does not predict the precise form such rivalry will take.

The preceding comments do not imply that the only determinants of industrial performance are the trinity of structural variables discussed above. They do represent, however, the key elements found in most industries, those that have general explanatory value. In some industries, other structural variables may assume a paramount role. Perhaps most importantly, conventional market structure theory completely ignores certain potential consequences of business conglomeration. Yet an increasing share of American business is done by conglomerate enterprises of this character. Let us therefore consider briefly some of the theoretical aspects of this form of business organization.

Business Conglomeration

As noted above, the market structure model attempts to predict the extent of a concern's market power, the explanation running in terms of how certain factors found in a *particular* market impose constraints on its behavior. But if a concern operates across many markets or industries, its behavior may not be subject to the competitive discipline of any one market. Hence, the extent of company conglomeration may well be an important element of market structure in some industries, because it permits competitive strategies not available to other companies.

Economists have identified a number of unique advantages inherent in company conglomeration. Corwin Edwards, for example, explains eloquently the advantages conferred by the sheer volume of a concern's resources:

> In encounters with small enterprises it can buy scarce materials and attractive sites, inventions, and facilities; preempt the services of the most expensive technicians and executives; and acquire reserves of materials for the future. It can absorb losses that would consume the entire capital of a smaller rival. . . . Moment by moment the big company can outbid, outspend, or outlose the small one; and from a series of such momentary advantages it derives an advantage in attaining its large aggregate results.[5]

Conglomeration can also sap the vigor of competition among fellow oligopolists themselves. When two or more conglomerates meet in many markets, they are likely to view one another with circumspection, recognizing full well that to press

[5] "Conglomerate Business as a Source of Power," in *Business Concentration and Price Policy* (New York: National Bureau of Economic Research, 1955), pp. 334–335.

an advantage today in one area may boomerang in another market tomorrow. The result may well be "a live and let live" attitude.

Smaller enterprises whose fortunes depend upon success in a single market may well decide that it is the better part of valor to behave less aggressively in their encounters with the conglomerate giants. They recognize that the multimarket conglomerate enterprise is in a position "to hurt without being hurt."

Finally, the conglomerate, because it produces many products, can engage in reciprocal selling, a sales strategy not generally open to the nonconglomerate enterprise. The promise "I'll buy from you if you'll buy from me" can be a powerful sales magnet.

In these and other ways, the conglomerate concern can attain and employ market power. Economists are not agreed, however, as to the exact extent of advantage conferred by conglomeration. Some economists reason that bigness and multimarket operations alone are not enough. Most probably agree, however, that when a conglomerate possesses market power in some areas, that power can become a vehicle for the enhancement of its power in other areas. Profits in one field can be used to subsidize expansion elsewhere, and the power to rebuff potential entrants may itself create barriers to entry. Hence, the significance of conglomeration is related to the concepts of market power discussed above, concentration and barriers to entry.

What are the theoretical limits to the growth of business conglomeration? Edwin G. Nourse makes the pessimistic prediction that there may be no natural market forces which contain its further expansion. As he puts it, "There are no demonstrable or discernible limits at which such concentration of economic power, once fully underway, would automatically cease." [6]

6 "Government Discipline of Private Economic Power," in *Administered Prices: A Compendium on Public Policy* (Washington, D.C.: Senate Subcommittee on Antitrust and Monopoly, 88th Cong., 1st Sess., 1963), p. 255.

NONMARKET FORCES AND BUSINESS BEHAVIOR

While the theory of monopoly explains how the organization of the market determines or influences business behavior, it must not be inferred that market forces alone determine how businesses act. Forces outside the market also have an impact, sometimes a decisive one. Some of these are internal to the business enterprise, for example, the peculiar whims or aspirations of individual business managers. Certainly the goals and the values of the elder Henry Ford had a decisive impact on the American automobile industry during its first decades. Other influences, including some that are external to both the business enterprise and the market within which it operates, for example, public policy toward business, frequently have a significant effect on behavior. It is sometimes said, and not without some justification, that the ghost of Senator John Sherman—author of the Sherman Antitrust Act of 1890—sits in the board room of all our larger corporations. Moreover, the level of industry demand, always the single most important short-run factor determining an industry's output, prices, and profits, is heavily influenced by the level of aggregate demand in the economy as a whole.

Although a diversity of these nonmarket forces can weigh heavily in the calculus of particular business decisions, the pervasive influence of the basic market forces are never completely muted. And, on close inspection, even seemingly nonmarket forces frequently are related to the nature of competition in the market. For example, only when a concern has substantial market power does management have sufficient discretion to engage in pricing and other actions satisfying its own personal gratifications. Where competitive market forces are keen, the business maverick who operates his business in an "uneconomic" manner will soon fall by the way.

Similarly, although national monetary and fiscal policy can

and does have a direct impact on the level of industry demand, the effectiveness of such policies can be dulled by noncompetitive industrial structures, a problem specifically dealt with in Chapter 7.

So much for the discussion of some of the theoretical concepts used in the probing of questions of market power. We turn now from the world of theory to the world of reality.

What are the patterns of market structure in American industry and how are they changing? What technological and market forces are responsible for existing structures? These are the questions the following three chapters attempt to answer.

CHAPTER 3

Concentration of
Economic Power

Because market power has many dimensions, it eludes capture by a single statistic. It has been seen how the level of concentration in a single industry is relevant to measuring the degree of oligopoly. On the other hand, preoccupation with concentration in individual industries ignores any potential power associated with vast resources and company conglomeration. Economists therefore use a variety of measures to probe the level of industrial concentration.

This chapter follows several approaches. It first measures so-called *aggregate concentration*. This measure is concerned with the extent to which total productive capacity and financial resources in a broad segment of the economy are controlled by a relatively few large corporations. The second measure deals with *market* or *industry concentration*. This measure refers to the share of an industry controlled by the leading producers of the product. Finally, a bridge is built between the levels of aggregate concentration and market concentration. Subsequent chapters probe the causes and the consequences of industrial concentration.

The comparisons deal mainly with the industrial sector of the economy. Not only are data most complete in this area, but it is the single most important sector of the economy. About one-third of the national wealth of the United States originates in the manufacturing sector; competition in related raw material and distribution industries are often influenced by the level of market power in manufacturing; the country especially depends on this sector for much technological progress and economic growth. Manufacturing and mining companies make nearly half of all business expenditures for new plants and equipment, earn half of all corporate profits, and account for 98 percent of all private research and development.

The current distribution of financial control in American industry has its roots in the great consolidation movement around the turn of the century. American manufacturing increased threefold between 1860 and 1890. Yet all manufacturing industries were made up of numerous small enterprises, and no truly large manufacturing company had emerged.

During the two decades around 1900 swift and irreversible changes occurred in most leading industries. For example, in 1889 the Carnegie steel interests had a capitalization of only $12.5 million. Yet within two decades Carnegie would become part of the largest corporation in the world. Carnegie expanded manyfold during the 1890s, until by 1900 it was recapitalized for $300 million. At the same time, other large steel companies were emerging through a series of consolidations. In 1901 the United States Steel Corporation was created out of a "combination of combinations." The new enterprise had a capitalization of $1.4 billion and controlled about 65 percent of all steel production. Although its stock was considerably watered, the company was the largest manufacturing enterprise of its day. Even in 1909, after many other large corporations had followed the merger route, United States Steel had assets as great as the combined assets of the next ten largest industrial corporations.

What occurred in steel was duplicated in other important industries. By 1909 American Tobacco, Standard Oil, du Pont, and American Can held from 60 to 90 percent of the business in their respective industries. The transformation of these and other industries marked the beginning of oligopolistic market structures in the American economy. Not only did the great consolidation movement result in oligopoly or near monopoly, but it also marked the beginning of many of our contemporary giant corporations. Already ranking among the top ten industrial corporations in 1909 were such prominent companies as United States Steel (1), Standard Oil of New Jersey (2), American Tobacco (3), International Harvester (5), Anaconda Copper (6), and Armour & Company (8), all of which are still leaders today.

Some great trusts of 1909 were subsequently partially dismantled by antitrust decrees; others lost their dominant positions to a second tier of companies. But in no industry has there been a return to the fragmented structures of the 1880s. The great merger movement around the turn of the century ushered in an era of oligopoly and big business, which have remained as permanent features on the industrial landscape.

Although considered big business in their day, all but a few companies were pigmies by comparison with today's large industrial complexes. For example, in 1909 only two corporations—Standard Oil (N.J.) and United States Steel—had assets in excess of $300 million. By 1969 there were eighty-seven manufacturing corporations with assets in excess of $1 billion.

It is difficult to grasp fully the transformation that has occurred in the size structure of American industry since the end of the nineteenth century. For example, in 1968, the three largest industrial corporations had combined sales of $53 billion. This was greater (after adjustments for changes in the price level) than America's gross national product at the time of the Civil War; more than the combined sales of the 204,750 manufacturing establishments recorded by the Census of Manufactures for 1899; and larger than the gross national product of all but nine of the 150-odd nations of the world.

AGGREGATE CONCENTRATION TRENDS

The level of aggregate concentration in American manufacturing has risen substantially since World War II. (Although prewar data are not precise, the largest industrial companies also expanded their share of corporate assets between 1909 and 1948.)[1] Table 3.1 shows the change in industrial concentration

TABLE 3.1 / SHARE OF MANUFACTURING CORPORATION ASSETS HELD BY THE 200 LARGEST CORPORATIONS, 1947–1968 (in percent)

Year	100 largest	200 largest
1947	39.3	47.2
1950	39.8	47.7
1955	44.2	53.1
1960	46.4	56.2
1965	46.5	56.6
1967	49.3	60.9

SOURCE: Federal Trade Commission, *Staff Report on Corporate Mergers,* 1969.

between 1947 and 1968, using the total assets of firms engaged in manufacturing as a measure of financial resources. By this measure, the share held by the top one hundred companies rose from 39.3 percent to 49.3 percent, and the share of the top 200 rose from 47.2 percent to 60.9 percent. In other words, by 1968 the top one hundred companies held a greater share than that held by the top 200 in 1947.

This substantial growth in industrial concentration occurred in the face of enormous growth in the economy. In fact, the total number of manufacturing corporations actually in-

1 Norman R. Collins and Lee E. Preston, "The Size Structure of the Largest Industrial Firms," *American Economic Review* (December 1961), p. 989.

creased by about 55,000 during the period. Thus this galaxy of a relatively few very large companies expanded its share in a universe that was itself expanding rapidly during the period.

Table 3.2 illustrates the degree to which financial resources had by 1969 become concentrated among a few hundred manufacturing corporations. Measured in terms of assets, just

TABLE 3.2 / CONCENTRATION OF ASSETS AND PROFITS IN AMERICAN MANUFACTURING INDUSTRIES, FIRST QUARTER OF 1969

Asset Size		TOTAL ASSETS	TOTAL NET PROFITS
Billions	*Corporations*	*Percent*	*Percent*
$1,000 and over	87	46	50
250–$1,000	206	20	19
100– 250	276	8	8
10– 100	2,024	13	11
Under 10	192,000*	14	12
Total	194,593	100 †	100

* Estimate.   † Rounded.

SOURCE: Federal Trade Commission and Securities and Exchange Commission, *Quarterly Financial Report for Manufacturing Corporations* (First Quarter, 1969), p. 61.

eighty-seven corporations, each with assets of over $1 billion, controlled 46 percent of the assets of all manufacturing corporations. Just over 500 corporations, each with assets exceeding $100 million, controlled 74 percent of such assets. This is a minimum estimate of the level of aggregate concentration; it does not take into account the fact that some large companies are actually owned or controlled by others. Moreover, some are joint ventures owned by the largest companies. These corporations control many domestic and foreign subsidiary corporations that hold billions of dollars in assets; they are only partially included in the figures shown in Table 3.2.

Perhaps the most significant indication of concentration of financial power is the concentration of profit. By this measure concentration is even higher than it is when measured in terms of assets. Whereas the top eighty-seven corporations controlled about 46 percent of all corporate manufacturing assets, they controlled about 50 percent of the net profits of such corporations (Table 3.2).

In general, then, while many thousands of manufacturing corporations exist, a privileged few control practically all manufacturing facilities and other resources. The great bulk of American manufacturing is done by just over 2,500 companies with assets of $10 million or more (Table 3.2). By 1968 these companies controlled 86 percent of the assets and earned 88 percent of the profits of all manufacturing corporations. While the remaining 192,000 corporations, plus numerous partnerships and proprietorships (about 175,000), still played an important role in some industries, most operated on the periphery of the industrial sphere. Many were essentially satellites living in the shadows of the industrial giants.

Although there have been shifts, entries, and exits among the companies occupying the top positions over the past half century, the extent of such mobility has declined in recent decades. Evidently the largest companies are achieving increasingly secure positions at the top of the industrial pyramid. This increasing stability at the top is surprising, as entire new industries have been created and destroyed since the years preceding World War II.

On the basis of their extensive analysis of the size structure and mobility of leading industrial concerns, Collins and Preston concluded that "there is *considerable* reason to believe that firms now at the top of the industrial pyramid *are* more likely to remain than their predecessors. The evidence of mobility *does* accord with a general assumption that large-scale corporations enjoy an increasing amount of entrenchment of position by virtue of their size." [2] They concluded that since

2 *Ibid.*, p. 1001.

the turn of the century equality of opportunity has decreased substantially in the upper reaches of the economy.

In sum, the United States depends upon a few hundred companies to carry on the great bulk of the country's manufacturing operations. Although nearly 400,000 companies, including proprietorships, partnerships and corporations, qualify as manufacturing companies, financial resources have become highly centralized among a few hundred concerns. Although size and financial wealth are not to be equated with monopoly power, the concentration of financial resources necessarily permeates many aspects of industrial performance. Ready access to vast resources enables an enterprise to engage in adventures not open to lesser enterprises.

Vast economic power is a fact of modern industrial life. The purpose here is not to lament this power but to understand it better. Quite clearly the country's top 200, 500, or 1,000 corporations are not going to wither in the decades ahead. On the contrary, recent trends suggest that they will hold or even expand their share of total industrial activity.

Because of the dominance of these powerful companies in the industrial sector, they necessarily must be the wellsprings of most economic progress in the decades ahead. This fact immediately raises the question of how vast economic power can be channeled to serve the public interest in a private enterprise economy. Are the disciplining forces traditionally relied on in a free enterprise economy still operative? Or have they become so blunted by sheer economic power as to require alternative forms of social control?

MARKET CONCENTRATION

Before turning to these questions of public policy, let us probe further into the anatomy of modern industrial structure to learn more about the nature and the sources of market power

—specifically, the level and the trend in *market* or *industrial concentration*. This measure refers to the share of an industry's business held by a few companies and is in contrast to the measures of *aggregate* concentration dealt with above. Instead of measuring concentration of all manufacturing assets or sales, it measures sales concentration in the manufacture of a particular product. Although aggregate concentration and product concentration may be related and each may have a bearing on "economic power," they do not necessarily move in the same direction.

Industrial or market concentration is directly related to matters of competition and monopoly. It shows where an industry is located in the broad spectrum between competition and monopoly. Economic theory suggests, and industrial experience verifies, that when industry sales are concentrated in few hands, rivals behave more like monopolists than competitors.

It has been seen that the degree of aggregate concentration has grown despite the enormous growth of the economy, including both the addition of entirely new industries—automobiles, electronics, man-made fibers, airplanes, and aerospace, to name a few—and an immense growth of existing ones. But what have been the trends in industry concentration since 1900? Unfortunately, inadequate data and great changes in the industry mix prevent precise measurement of trends in industrial concentration before 1947. However, the best available estimates suggest that, on balance, there was no clear-cut movement in either direction. Concentration declined in some industries and rose in others.

Much better information is available for the period 1947–1966, but here again the pattern is mixed. Although, as shown earlier, aggregate concentration clearly rose since World War II, there has been no clear-cut trend toward either an increase or a decrease in market concentration. Industries experiencing increases in concentration were almost precisely offset by industries experiencing declines. This conclusion is based on the analysis of 213 representative industries. Of these industries, the share of business done by the top four firms rose in eighty-eight industries, dropped in seventy-eight, and remained the same in forty-seven (Table 3.3). (These so-called "four-digit census industries" consist of all plants primarily engaged in the production of a given group of closely related products.) Although more industries experienced increases than decreases in concentration, when industries are weighed by their size, the decreases exceed the increases (Appendix Table A3).

These overall figures suggest a rather high degree of stability in market concentration trends, while inspection of the various industry groupings indicates divergent trends. First, an appearance of overall stability results because a modest decrease in average four-firm concentration between 1947 and 1958 was offset by an almost identical increase between 1958 and 1966 (Appendix Table A4). Second, whereas four-firm concentration was relatively stable between 1947 and 1966, eight-firm concentration rose persistently during the entire period (Appendix Tables A3 and A4). Third, and most important, the consumer goods industries manifested a persistent trend toward rising concentration, whereas producer goods industries tended to decline. (Producer goods are sold mainly to other manufacturers or service industry companies; consumer goods are ultimately sold to households for personal use.) Of 132 producer goods industries, concentration rose in forty-one, declined in sixty, and remained the same in thirty-one. On the other hand, in the consumer goods industries four-firm concentration rose in forty-seven industries, declined in eighteen, and remained about the same in sixteen (Table 3.3). The consumer goods industries experiencing increasing concentration covered a broad spectrum of products including dog and cat foods, cereal preparations, chewing gum, coffee, cigars, corsets, household refrigerators, TV receivers, and motor vehicles.

The rising concentration in consumer goods industries reflects the growing importance of large-scale advertising and promotion in the postwar years. (As discussed in the following chapter, advertising-achieved product differentiation represents the major source of market concentration in many industries.)

TABLE 3.3 / CHANGES IN FOUR-FIRM CONCENTRATION IN 213 INDUSTRIES, 1947–1966

Type of Industry	Total	NUMBER OF INDUSTRIES WHERE FOUR-FIRM CONCENTRATION		
		Increased	Remained the Same *	Decreased
All industries	213	88	47	78
Producer goods	132	41	31	60
Consumer goods	81	47	16	18

* Change less than 3 percentage points.

SOURCE: "Industrial Structure and Competition Policy," in *Studies by the Staff of the Cabinet Committee on Price Stability* (January 1969), p. 59.

Significantly, there are divergent patterns within the consumer goods industries, depending on the character of products. Concentration rose most persistently in industries whose products were "highly differentiated" through advertising and promotion. Examples of such products are breakfast cereals and household detergents. Conversely, in consumer industries where products were relatively "undifferentiated," concentration tended to decline. Examples of such products are fresh meats and butter. These contrasting patterns within the consumer goods industries are shown in Table 3.4.

But what about the producer goods industries experiencing decreasing concentration? It will come as a surprise to many that, on balance, market concentration declined outside the consumers goods fields. Four-firm concentration declined in sixty producer-goods industries and increased in forty-one. Among the important such industries experiencing declines in concentration were chemicals, fabricated metal, and machinery. But, as noted above, this trend may have been reversed in recent years.

Quite clearly, different economic forces were at work in consumer goods industries than in other industries. The economic

TABLE 3.4 / CHANGE IN FOUR-FIRM CONCENTRATION IN CONSUMER GOODS INDUSTRIES, 1947–1966

	PERCENT OF INDUSTRIES WHERE CONCENTRATION	
Type of Industry	*Increased*	*Decreased*
Highly differentiated products	88	12
Moderately differentiated products	65	35
Undifferentiated products	57	43

SOURCE: "Industrial Structure and Competition Policy," in *Studies by the Staff of the Cabinet Committee on Price Stability* (Washington, D.C.: January 1969), p. 59.

causes underlying these developments are discussed in the next chapter.

Suffice it to say here that powerful countervailing forces are at work, the net effect of these forces being to erode concentration in some industries and increase it in others. The experience of the past sixty years proves that there is nothing inherent in twentieth-century American capitalism that makes increasing market concentration and monopoly inevitable. This is not to imply that there is not a concentration problem in American manufacturing. On the contrary, a number of extremely important industries are very concentrated and have remained so for many years. Table 3.5 lists twenty-seven of the most concentrated American industries. In these industries the top four firms controlled 60 percent or more of sales in one or more years between 1947 and 1963. (The one industry listed in Table 3.5 with sales under 60 percent in either 1947 or 1963 had over 60 percent of sales in 1954.) These twenty-seven high-concentration industries had sales of over $40 billion in 1966 and represent the core of the oligopoly problem in America. In each of these industries oligopolistic interdependence is high, and oligopolistic pricing in most is shielded by high barriers to

TABLE 3.5 / TWENTY-SEVEN HIGHLY CONCENTRATED MANU-
FACTURING INDUSTRIES

| | FOUR-FIRM MARKET SHARE | | |
Producer Goods Industries	1947 (percent)	1963 (percent)	Change
Locomotives and parts	91	97	+ 6
Flat glass	90	94	+ 4
Gypsum products	85	84	− 1
Primary copper	83	78	− 5
Salt	81	77	− 4
Explosives	80	72	− 8
Typewriters	79	76	− 3
Tin cans	78	74	− 4
Synthetic fibers	78	81	+ 3
Transformers	73	68	− 5
Aircraft engines	72	56	− 16
Cane sugar refining	70	62	− 8
Computers	69	63	− 6
Tractors	67	69	+ 2
Engine electric equipment	67	69	+ 2
Elevators	63	62	− 1
Ball and roller bearings	62	57	− 5
Railway and street cars	56	53	− 3
Consumer Goods Industries			
Electric lamps	92	92	0
Cigarettes	90	80	− 10
Hard surface flooring	80	87	+ 7
Soap and glycerine	79	90	+ 11
Cereal preparations	79	86	+ 7
Tires and tubes	77	76	− 1
Photographic equipment	61	63	+ 2
Motor vehicles and parts	56	79	+ 23
Domestic laundry equipment	40	78	+ 38

SOURCE: Based on William G. Sheppard, "Evidence about Market Power,"
Antitrust Bulletin (Spring 1967), p. 67.

entry. Hence neither actual nor potential competitors provide much stimulus for price competition. But, importantly, market concentration declined between 1947 and 1963 in thirteen of the eighteen producer goods industries shown in Table 3.5. In contrast, concentration rose in seven of the nine consumer goods industries shown. These patterns are consistent with the findings noted above concerning the downward drift in concentration in producer goods industries and an upward movement in consumer goods industries.

It cannot be emphasized too strongly that these industries are not representative of the total manufacturing industry, and certainly not of all American industry. The industries shown in Table 3.5 accounted for only about 15 percent of the sales of all manufacturing. Most unregulated nonmanufacturing industries are less concentrated than are manufacturing industries. (The service and distributive trades, which account for about 26 percent of national income, generally are more competitively structured than are manufacturing industries.) Most manufacturing industries are relatively unconcentrated. Table 3.6 distributes 382 census manufacturing industries (the four-digit census industries—see page 31) by the share of business done by the top four companies in 1966. In 67 percent of these industries the top four companies did less than 50 percent of the business. In only 9 percent of the industries did the top four do 75 percent or more of the business; and in another 24 percent, the top four did from 50 percent to 74 percent of the business.

Although these data tend to understate somewhat the actual level of market concentration in manufacturing,[3] it is clear that the great bulk of manufacturing is carried on in industries

---

[3] The data suffer from several defects. First, in some cases the industry classifications tend to be too broad. For example, all canned fruits and vegetables are defined as a single industry. Second, the table does not include local or regional industries, such as fluid milk processing and baking, which generally are quite highly concentrated. On the other hand, the figures do not include imports, with the result that concentration is overstated in some industries. Similarly, the products of some industries are competitive with one another.

TABLE 3.6 / DISTRIBUTION OF MANUFACTURING INDUSTRIES BY FOUR-FIRM CONCENTRATION-RATION QUARTILES, 1966

Level of Four-Firm Concentration	INDUSTRIES		VALUE OF SHIPMENTS	
	Number	Percent	Total (billions)	Percent
75%–100%	33	9%	$ 66	14%
50%–74%	90	24	89	19
25%–49%	154	40	40	40
Under 24%	105	27	124	27
Total	382	100%	$319	100%

SOURCE: "Industrial Structure and Competition Policy," in *Studies by the Staff of the Cabinet Committee on Price Stability* (Washington, D.C.: January 1969), p. 57.

which are quite competitively structured. As will be discussed in Chapter 4, empirical studies demonstrate that market power of firms is quite limited in industries in which the top four firms control less than 40 percent of industry production. This suggests that competition is quite intense in well over one-half of American manufacturing industries.

A final word about the paradox of increasing *overall concentration* and rather stable trend in *market concentration*. As noted at the beginning of this chapter, the share of total manufacturing done by the top 200 firms rose substantially between 1947 and 1968. Yet it has just been observed that the average level of *market concentration* remained quite stable over the period. The explanation for this seeming contradiction is to be found partly in the growing conglomeration of large corporations. Since World War II the largest corporations have entered many new industries, usually by acquiring established concerns. Entry by merger does not have an immediate impact on market concentration, although it does increase the share of total manufacturing done by the largest concerns. Consequently, the increasing conglomeration of

American industry contributed to increasing overall concentration, but did not result in immediate widespread increases in market concentration.

The growing conglomeration of industry involved more than merely the increase of size flowing from growing diversification. As industrial concerns became increasingly conglomerated, they achieved *leading* positions in more and more industries. This is illustrated by Table 3.7. Whereas in 1958,

TABLE 3.7 / NUMBER OF THE FOUR LEADING INDUSTRY POSITIONS HELD BY COMPANIES RANKING AMONG THE 100 LARGEST MANUFACTURERS, 1958 AND 1963

Number of Leading Positions Held	NUMBER OF COMPANIES	
	1958	*1963*
20 or more	2	3
10–20	5	14
7– 9	14	21
4– 6	22	32
4 or more	43	70
Only 1	18	7
None	5	0
Total	100	100

SOURCE: Federal Trade Commission, *Staff Report on Corporate Mergers,* 1969, Table 4–1.

twenty-nine of the one hundred largest manufacturers were included among the four leading sellers in four or more industries, by 1963, seventy of these companies were among the four leaders in four or more industries. Since 1963 the number of leading positions occupied by these companies has increased even more because of their numerous mergers (see Chapter 5).

Not only do a few hundred large companies occupy the leading positions in many industries, but they are particularly prevalent in the most highly concentrated industries. One study of 135 manufacturing industries showed that the 200 largest companies did 87 percent of the business in industries where four-firm market concentration exceeded 75 percent. In contrast, these companies did only 14 percent of the business in industries where four-firm concentration was under 25 percent (see Table 3.8).

TABLE 3.8 / SHARE OF INDUSTRY HELD BY THE TOP 200 MANUFACTURERS IN 135 INDUSTRIES, 1963

Level of Four-Firm Concentration	Share of Industry Held by Top 200
76%–100%	87%
51%– 75%	63%
25%– 50%	31%
under 25%	14%

SOURCE: "Industrial Structure and Competition Policy," in *Studies by the Staff of the Cabinet Committee on Price Stability* (January 1969), p. 59.

These facts show that the largest companies have increased not only their share of all manufacturing business, but they have increased both the breadth and depth of their economic power base.

OTHER SOURCES OF CENTRALIZED
ECONOMIC POWER

In addition to the sources of economic power already discussed, there exist various more subtle intercorporate linkages that actually or potentially centralize corporate decision making. Here we shall discuss only the most important of these: increasing numbers of joint ventures and management ties among large concerns; the growing interconnections between banks and other business enterprises; and a growing concentration of financial control outside the industrial sector of the economy.

Corporate Management Interlocks

The corporation is a legal creation of the state, an artificial being with legal rights and obligations. Its activities, of course, are conducted by mere mortals. Its day-to-day operations are carried on under the direction of its chief executive officers, usually the corporate president and a chairman of the board. These officials, in turn, are accountable to a board of directors, who in theory are elected by the stockholders, the legal owners of the corporation. Because stockholdings are greatly diffused in the large modern corporation, there is, in practice, a sharp separation between ownership and control. The result is that the chief executive officers and the members of the board are in de facto control of most large corporations.

The potential for control over corporate decisions is broadened when corporate officers and directors sit on the boards of two or more corporations. Although the antitrust laws (see Chapter 9) prevent directors from being on the boards of companies that are *direct competitors,* no such restriction is placed on director interlocks among companies that occupy a buyer-seller relationship or that are *potential competitors.* Neither does existing law prohibit corporate *officers* from serving on the boards of direct competitors.

A recent Congressional staff study of the twenty largest industrial companies showed that in 1962 they had officer and director interlocks with 498 other industrial corporations, 235 financial institutions, ninety-five insurance companies, and thirty-two other corporations.[4] Frequently the interlocks were among the nation's largest corporations. For example, General

4 "Interlocks in Corporate Management" (Washington, D.C.: U.S. House of Representatives, Staff Report to the Antitrust Subcommittee of the Committee on the Judiciary, March 12, 1965), p. 117.

Motors, the largest private industrial corporation, was interlocked with sixty-three companies with combined assets exceeding $65 billion, including the country's largest railroad (The Pennsylvania) and the largest telephone company (American Telephone and Telegraph). The eighty-nine companies interlocked with the United States Steel Corporation had combined assets exceeding $100 billion.

Many leading companies are interlocked with suppliers, customers, or potential competitors. For example, there are automobile companies which are interlocked with steel, tire, aluminum, and copper companies.

Although such management interlocks have been commonplace for decades, they take on added significance today because of the growing concentration of economic activity among a relatively few corporations. Increasingly, these great enterprises are the chief actual or potential competitors of one another in many parts of the economy. Management interlocks therefore hold the potential for further centralization of corporate decision making over vital segments of the economy.

Corporate Joint Ventures

Jointly owned business enterprises represent a more intimate centralization of corporate decision making than do management interlocks. The creation of a jointly owned business by two or more corporations involves a partial merging of interests, a decision to develop an area jointly rather than independently. Although not a new phenomenon, in recent decades corporate joint ventures have grown in prominence and have assumed added significance because of the growing relative importance of the largest companies.

A recent study by Stanley Boyle shows that in 1965 the 500 largest industrial companies appeared 518 times as parents of joint ventures.[5] The top one hundred companies were espe-

[5] Stanley E. Boyle, "An Estimate of the Number and Size Distribution

cially prominent among these parents, accounting for 210 of the total. And especially important, in most cases the top one hundred corporations were linked with companies found among the top 500 industrial corporations.

Over half of the joint ventures were owned by parents that produced identical or closely related products; hence, they frequently united direct competitors. Because competitive performance in manufacturing increasingly depends on the behavior of the leading 200 or so companies, joint ventures among these and other leading concerns, like management interlocks, may dampen their competitive spirit. Partnerships in one area of interest may discourage independent behavior in other fields. Nor is this idle theory. Walter Mead of the University of California has shown that joint ventures have indeed reduced competitive rivalry in some parts of the petroleum industry.[6]

Control by Bank Trust Departments

During most of the first half of this century there appears to have been a trend toward a diminution of control by commercial banks over nonfinancial businesses. Increasingly, large corporations grew by retained earnings or by printing their own money, in effect; that is, they issued new stocks and other kinds of financial obligations when buying new companies or adding new capacity. The ability to grow in these ways tended to erode the influence that commercial banking held over much of the industrial economy in the late nineteenth and early twentieth centuries.

A recent development, almost entirely a product of the last two decades, promises to reverse this diminishing influence of

---

of Domestic Joint Subsidiaries," *Antitrust Law and Economic Review* (Spring 1968), p. 86.

[6] Walter Mead, "The Competitive Significance of Joint Ventures," *The Antitrust Bulletin* (Fall 1967), pp. 819–49.

banks over nonfinancial corporations. Since World War II more and more corporations and other institutions have established pension funds. Typically these funds are placed in trust with commercial banks.[7] In the short space of twelve years, between 1955 and 1967, pension fund assets grew nearly four-fold, from $25 billion to $100 billion. It is predicted that within another eleven years such assets will grow to $285 billion, with $200 billion of this placed in bank trust departments. In addition to pension funds, many individuals, estates, and institutions place their investments in bank trust departments. By 1967 bank trust departments managed investments with a market value of $250 billion, nearly two-thirds of which was invested in stocks of private corporations.

Most trust department assets are held by forty-nine of the 3,100 banks with such departments. These forty-nine banks, individually, held 5 percent or more of outstanding shares of stock in 5,270 companies. The banks act as sole trustee for about 80 percent of the funds that they manage. Because stock ownership is widely dispersed in nearly all large corporations, a bank with 5 percent or more of a company's voting stock has considerable potential for control over crucial corporate decisions. Such potential control is frequently reinforced by inter-locking directorships between banks and corporations. In 1967 the forty-nine banks referred to had directors on the boards of 6,591 other corporations.

Some banks held substantial interests in numerous companies. Morgan Guaranty Trust Company (New York) held, in trust, 5 percent or more of the stock in 270 companies with combined assets exceeding $100 billion. It also had interlocking directorships with 233 companies.

Frequently banks' trust departments hold substantial stock interests in competing companies. Turning to Morgan Guar-

---

[7] Except where noted, the discussions in this section are based on *Commercial Banks and Their Trust Activities: Emerging Influence in the American Economy*, Vol. I (Washington, D.C.: U.S. Staff Report of the Subcommittee on Domestic Finance, Committee on Banking and Currency, July 8, 1968).

anty again, we find it held 5 percent of one or more classes of stock in nine nonferrous metal companies: Kennecott Copper Company, American Smelting & Refining Company, Phelps Dodge Corporation, Revere Copper & Brass Company, American Metal Climax, Incorporated, Kaiser Aluminum & Chemical Company, Alcan Aluminum, Limited, Scovill Manufacturing Company, and St. Joseph Lead Company.

Airlines illustrate the potential for centralized control over an entire industry by a few banks. In 1967, two New York City banks—Morgan Guaranty and Chase Manhattan—held 5 percent or more of the common stock in seven leading airlines. Morgan Guaranty's holdings were as follows: United Airlines, 8.2 percent; American Airlines, 7.5 percent; and T.W.A.; 7.5 percent. Chase Manhattan held stock in the following airlines: T.W.A., 7.8 percent; Eastern Airlines, 6.4 percent; Pan American Airlines, 6.7 percent; Northwest Airlines, 11.0 percent; and Western Airlines, 6.7 percent.

The inevitable concentration of more and more voting stock in the trust departments of commercial banks creates the specter of centralization of corporate decisions in the hands of a relatively few banks. On this point, Adolfe Berle has concluded:

> We thus dimly discern the outline of a permanently concentrated group of officials, holding a paramount and virtually unchallenged power position over the American industrial economy. . . . Tomorrow these centers will be able, without having to ask assistance from individual stockholders, to deliver a controlling vote at will.[8]

Centralization of Control Outside Manufacturing

The trend toward centralization of corporate control within manufacturing promises to extend to other parts of the econ-

---

[8] *Power without Property* (New York: Harcourt, Brace & World, 1959), pp. 55–56.

omy. The greatest potential source of such increased centralization are the recently created holding companies of leading banks and railroads.

National banks and most state banks are foreclosed from entering manufacturing, insurance, and other fields outside banking. An avenue of escape from these restrictions has been the formation of one-bank holding companies. Through this device, stockholders control their bank indirectly after exchanging shares in it for shares in a holding company. Although existing law prevents such holding companies from controlling more than one bank (hence their name), they may acquire businesses in other fields. Until recent years few large banks took advantage of this loophole in the law. Between July, 1967, and January, 1969, however, thirty-four of the one hundred largest commercial banks, with combined deposits of over $100 billion, formed or announced plans to form one-bank holding companies.[9] Included among these were the country's six largest banks. Already some one-bank holding companies operate in such disparate fields as insurance, mutual funds, railroads, manufacturing, and hospitals. Although still in its infancy, this development carries within it the seeds for an immense centralization of resources; for if large banks expand aggressively into other sectors, they have the financial resources to control vast parts of the economy.

Closely related to the one-bank holding company is the railroad holding company. Like banks, many railroads are seeking to expand outside of traditional lines by forming holding companies which purchase other lines of business. For example, the Chicago and North Western Railroad recently established a holding company called Northwest Industries. The latter controls a substantial volume of railroad properties, two chemical companies, and, since 1968, Universal Manufacturing Corporation, Lone Star Steel Company, Union Underwear Company, Imperial Reading Company, Fruit of the Loom, Inc., and Acme

[9] *The Growth of Unregistered Bank Holding Companies* (Washington, D.C.: U.S. Staff Report for the Committee on Banking and Currency, House of Representatives, February 11, 1969), p. 1.

Boat Company. Northwest is currently (1969) seeking to acquire the B. F. Goodrich Company. If they are successful in this latest bid, they will have become, in just two years, one of the nation's largest industrials. Similarly, Illinois Central Industries, a holding company created by the Illinois Central Railroad, has already acquired a foundry and a producer of heavy electrical equipment, and recently made a bid to acquire Abex, a manufacturer of railroad equipment with annual sales near $300 million. Recently the Penn Central Railroad, itself a product of the 1967 merger of the country's two leading railroads, created a holding company for the avowed purpose of aggressive diversification into new fields. Penn Central has announced its intention to embark on a widespread merger program financed by tax loss carry-forwards of from $500 million to $600 million. It has already acquired control of such diverse properties as a natural gas line to the Allied Chemical Building in New York, and control of a professional basketball team and hockey team. In late 1969 it announced its intention to buy two oil companies.

Large-scale merger-achieved expansion by railroads into new areas could further centralize corporate control over American industry. There is also a danger that such holding companies will drain their transportation facilities of the money needed for maintenance and modernization, thereby causing a further deterioration of customer services.

SUMMARY

This chapter has shown that *market concentration* declined modestly in the postwar years. Nonetheless, in a number of key industries, sales are held in the hands of a few sellers. A vital link is discernible connecting growing industrial conglomeration and aggregate concentration with existing high levels of market concentration. The typical conglomerate is not only large, but also operates in at least some industries where it holds market power. This power nourishes the conglomerate, thereby conferring potential economic advantage beyond that associated with sheer size alone. Several more subtle intercorporate relationships also exist that tend to centralize corporate decision making, and the number of such relationships has been increasing. Finally, recent developments in the banking, transportation, and communications industries, if unchecked, promise to obliterate traditional industrial boundaries and further concentrate corporate resources.

Before turning to the potential uses and implications of discretionary market power, let us probe the underlying causes of industrial concentration.

CHAPTER 4

Causes of Concentration

Why are some industries near monopolies and others atomistically structured? Why is concentration increasing in some industries and declining in others? What are the long-run prospects for maintaining a competitively structured economy? This chapter and the following one explore these questions.

An industry's structure is not determined by random events. It is a product of observable and measurable economic forces. Nor are these forces confined by national boundaries. For example, the match industry is highly concentrated in America, Great Britain, Canada, and most other Western nations. Similarly, two or three firms manufacture almost all the liquid detergents in Great Britain, Canada, and the United States. Steel, chemicals, and autos are highly concentrated in all Western nations, whereas services and trades are generally unconcentrated.

It is a mistake, however, to assume that the structures of all industries are entirely the products of an inescapable economic determinism. We will see how the structures of industries have been molded by private and public actions. Such actions are constrained, however, by certain fundamental economic and institutional forces. What are these?

The first generalization about the causes of industrial concentration is that there is no single explanation. A variety of complex—and sometimes conflicting—forces ultimately determine the level of concentration.

Economists have identified a number of economic factors playing an especially important role in determining or shaping the level of industrial concentration. Some of these relate to underlying economic and technical phenomena, particularly the advantages of large-scale production, invention and innovation, and promotion and distribution. These factors are the subject matter of this chapter.

(The following chapter deals with mergers as a special cause of concentration. While mergers are often related to basic economic causes, they are an especially unique form of growth because they can bring about rapid and irreversible changes in industry structure without being subjected to the same market tests imposed on internal growth.)

A variety of business practices in addition to mergers may have an important bearing on industry structure. Unrestrained price discrimination, predatory behavior, and related tactics may place small concerns at a serious competitive disadvantage. In such a situation market power replaces economic efficiency in determining industrial survival and growth. Although "unfair" competitive tactics are more difficult to detect and measure, a variety of more subtle such tactics may have a similar effect. Especially important in this respect may be certain competitive strategies available to the large conglomerate enterprise operating across many industries. (These various forms of market behavior and their consequences are discussed in some detail in Chapter 6.)

Finally, industrial history speaks eloquently of how public policy may create an environment that encourages or discourages the emergence of industrial concentration. (This subject will be dealt with in Chapter 9.)

LARGE-SCALE PRODUCTION

Some important research has been conducted into the extent to which large-scale economies dictate high concentration. The evidence is sharpest in economies of large-scale production. Production economies refer to the lower per unit costs resulting from mass production, use of specialized machinery, and employment of specialized supervisory personnel and management. Such economies are clearly distinguished from economies associated with large-scale distribution, invention, and innovation, subjects also discussed in this chapter.

Economies of large-scale production pose a serious public policy dilemma. In clear-cut cases where increasing returns to large-scale production dictate monopoly, such as in telephone service and electric power, the American answer has been either regulation or government ownership. But if increasing-returns industries prove the rule rather than the exception, a basic question about the compatibility of productive efficiency and a competitively structured economy is introduced. It is therefore extremely significant that recent research studies are unanimous in their conclusions that productive efficiency dictates high concentration in only a small—and declining—share of all manufacturing.

In his classic study of barriers to new competition, Bain found that economies of large-scale production did not explain high levels of concentration in very many industries[1]—not even in automobiles, where production economies are substantial. Most advantages of large-scale production are achieved by a plant manufacturing 300,000 automobiles a year, although additional economies may be achieved in plants making up to 600,000 units annually.

Experience bears out these estimates. American Motors had high profits in years when it enjoyed sales of around 400,000

[1] Joe S. Bain, *Barriers to New Competition* (Cambridge, Mass.: Harvard University Press, 1956).

units. Its problems in recent years have stemmed not from in-efficiency in production but from problems in distribution. As explained below, substantial economies may be achieved by large-scale distribution of automobiles.

In separate studies, Leonard W. Weiss and T. R. Saving analyzed statistically the "survivor" rate of various sized plants.[2] Both researchers concluded that the requirements of large-scale manufacturing plants do not explain existing levels of concentration in very many industries. Saving estimates that in over 70 percent of the 132 manufacturing industries for which he made estimates, minimum-sized efficient plants were equal to less than 1 percent of their respective industry's out-put. These industries accounted for over 83 percent of the total output produced in the sample of industries.

Another way of gauging the relation between production economies and concentration is to measure the divergence be-tween plant concentration and firm concentration. If produc-tion efficiency dictates industry concentration, each company would be expected to concentrate its output in a very few large plants. As a result, plant concentration would tend to approxi-mate company concentration. For example, if there are in-creasing economies of production over a very wide range, mo-nopoly would result, with the monopolist operating a single plant. Or, if four companies constitute an industry, each com-pany would operate only a single plant. Thus, when produc-tive efficiency is of paramount importance, there is little diver-gence between plant and company concentration.

The most authoritative work on this subject has been done by John M. Blair, chief economist of the Senate Subcommittee on Antitrust and Monopoly. His most recent study reveals two important facts.[3]

[2] T. R. Saving, "Estimation of Optimum Size Plant by the Survivor Technique," *Quarterly Journal of Economics* (November 1961), pp. 569–607; Leonard W. Weiss, "The Survival Technique and the Extent of Suboptional Capacity," *Journal of Political Economy* (June 1964), p. 246.

[3] *Economic Concentration* (Washington, D.C.: U.S. Senate, Hearings before the Subcommittee on Antitrust and Monopoly of the Committee

First, in most manufacturing industries there is a considerable divergence between plant and company concentration. For example, whereas in 1963 four *companies* produced 50 percent of all blast furnace and steel mill shipments, the four largest *plants* manufacturing these products made only 16 percent of such shipments. In metal can manufacturing the divergence is even greater. Whereas in 1963 eight *companies* sold 85 percent of all metal cans, the eight largest *plants* made only 16 percent of these. Perhaps most surprising is that in motor vehicles and parts the top four *companies* controlled 75 percent of the output, whereas the eight largest *plants* made only 16 percent of the total.

Second, in most industries the divergence between plant and company concentration has increased since World War II. For example, between 1947 and 1963 the share of industry shipments of the four largest metal can plants fell from 24 percent to 16 percent. These developments are extremely important in that they indicate that most markets are growing more rapidly than are the requirements of large-scale production.

In sum, in only a few industries is there strong support for the proposition that the requirements of large-scale production dictate a high level of concentration; moreover, the number of such industries has declined in recent years. As a result, if existing levels of concentration had originally been caused by the requirements of large-scale production, erosion of concentration could be predicted in many industries.

INVENTION AND INNOVATION

Some persons argue that economies of scale in research and innovation make high concentration and near monopoly an inevitable concomitant of modern capitalism. This doctrine,

on the Judiciary, 90th Cong., 1st Sess., Part VI, October 6, 1967), pp. 2970–2977.

originating in the speculations of Joseph Schumpeter and elaborated upon by his followers, holds that modern technology demands vast business concerns. At the very core of this new doctrine lies the assertion that only big companies can afford the large scientific and technical staffs dictated by modern technology. John K. Galbraith puts this thesis well when he asserts:

> There is no more pleasant fiction than that technical change is the product of the matchless ingenuity of the small man forced by competition to employ his wits to better his neighbor. Unhappily, it is fiction. Technical development has long since become the preserve of the scientist and the engineer. Most of the cheap and simple inventions have, to put it bluntly, been made. Not only is development now sophisticated and costly but it must be on a sufficient scale so that successes and failures will in some measure average out.[4]

This argument rests on the critical assumption that the technological imperatives of modern industrial organization dictate vast industrial organizations. So vast, Galbraith believes, that high levels of concentration and great market power are the inevitable result. It cannot be emphasized too strongly, however, that these are questions of fact rather than of theory.

Considerable evidence has been developed to test the Schumpeterian thesis. Although somewhat inconclusive, recent studies lend little comfort for this thesis. It is true that low-concentration industries such as apparel and furniture spend little on research; conversely, other low-concentration industries—scientific instruments, insecticides, and fungicides—spend considerable amounts. Experience also shows a mixed picture in industries of moderate-to-high concentration. Firms in some concentrated industries spend large amounts on research and development. Chemicals is a leading example. On the other hand, some very concentrated industries have tradi-

---

[4] *American Capitalism, the Concept of Countervailing Power* (Boston: Houghton Mifflin, 1952), p. 91.

tionally devoted insignificant amounts to invention and innovation—examples are cigarettes and linoleum. Even in concentrated industries with greater opportunities for research and innovation, the leading companies sometimes compare poorly in relation to their smaller members. The steel industry is a case in point.

After the creation of United States Steel in 1901, the American steel industry fit snugly in the Schumpeterian model. Yet the leading steel companies have had a lackluster record as inventive and innovative forces in this most basic industry. The accomplishments of United States Steel have been especially disappointing. After thorough study of the corporation, an engineering consulting firm reported to United States Steel in 1939 that the company was lagging badly in many respects. George W. Stocking summarized the findings thus:

> Ford, Bacon and Davis, the engineers whose findings corroborated the findings of the corporation's own engineers, pictured the corporation as a big, sprawling, inert giant, whose production operations were improperly coordinated; suffering from the lack of a long-run planning agency; relying on an antiquated system of cost accounting; with an inadequate knowledge of the cost or of the relative profitability of the many thousands of items it sold; with production and cost standards generally below those considered everyday practice in other industries; with inadequate knowledge of its domestic markets and no clear appreciation of its opportunities in foreign markets; with less efficient production facilities than those of its rivals; slow in introducing new processes and new products.[5]

These findings concerning what had been the world's greatest industrial corporation for decades represent a serious indictment of the Schumpeterian thesis. Nor has United States Steel or any other large steel company performed much better

[5] *Basing Point Pricing and Regional Development* (Chapel Hill, N.C.: University of North Carolina Press, 1954), p. 141.

since 1939. A study made by Daniel Hamberg of the thirteen major innovations in the American steel industry between 1940 and 1955 (ten after 1950) reveals that none was the outgrowth of American companies.[6] Four innovations were based on inventions of European steel companies (generally small by American standards), and seven came from independent inventors.

Especially instructive is the record of the oxygen steelmaking process introduced by dominant American steel companies.[7] The basic oxygen process has been called the only major technological breakthrough at the ingot level of steelmaking since before 1900.

Big Steel not only played no role in the discovery and initial development of this important process, but it also lagged in introducing it. A small Austrian steel company (which was one-third the size of a single plant of United States Steel) perfected and introduced the oxygen process. The first American company to adopt the new process, in 1954, was McLouth Steel, which had less than 1 percent of industry capacity. Although other small companies followed McLouth's lead, not until 1964 did the country's two leading steel companies, United States Steel and Bethlehem, introduce the process. This was fully ten years after McLouth, and fourteen years after the small pioneering Austrian firm, had introduced this revolutionary process.

Of course, theories can be neither proven nor disproven by a single case study. But other persuasive evidence shows that large companies have not contributed their proportionate share of important inventions. A study of the origin of sixty-one major inventions made between 1900 and 1955 reveals that only twelve originated in the research laboratories of large

[6] Statement by Dr. Daniel Hamberg, in *Concentration, Invention, and Innovation* (Washington, D.C.: U.S. Senate, Hearings before the Subcommittee on Antitrust and Monopoly of the Committee on the Judiciary, 89th Cong., 1st Sess., Part III, May 1965), p. 1287.

[7] Walter Adams and Joel B. Dirlam, "Big Steel, Invention, and Innovation," *Quarterly Journal of Economics* (May 1966), p. 167.

corporations.[8] Lone inventors and small research organizations played a big role even in the latter part of the period.

F. M. Scherer recently completed an extensive statistical analysis of the relation between market power and inventive success. He found that while inventive output increases with size of company, it does so at a less than proportionate rate. Nor did he find any systematic relation between the degree of market power and inventive success. Scherer concluded: "These findings among other things raise doubts whether the big, monopolistic conglomerate corporation is as efficient an engine of technological change as disciples of Schumpeter (including the author) have supposed it to be. Perhaps a bevy of fact-mechanics can still rescue the Schumpeter engine from disgrace, but at present the outlook seems pessimistic." [9]

Although large size is not a necessary prerequisite to invention, substantial resources are often required to put an invention to work. But even here the biggest companies have not always been most successful. Edwin Mansfield's careful study of innovation patterns shows a mixed pattern. Although the largest concerns in some industries have excelled, those in others have lagged. Perhaps most important, however, is the mixed evidence. It strongly suggests that factors other than sheer size determine the innovative record of a company. Apparently a company's attitude toward the innovative process is more important than its financial capacity to innovate.

Thus, while the Schumpeterian thesis has some empirical support, the weight of the evidence clearly contradicts the assertion that the imperatives of modern research and development (R&D) costs dictate monopoly or near monopoly. Schumpeter failed to anticipate that most American industries would support many companies capable of innovating. Whereas in the 1930s, when Schumpeter was writing, fewer

[8] John Jewkes, David Sawers, and Richard Stillerman, *The Sources of Invention* (New York: Macmillan, 1958).

[9] F. M. Scherer, "Firm Size, Market Structure, Opportunity, and the Output of Patented Inventions," *American Economic Review* (December 1965), pp. 1121–1122.

than one hundred industrial concerns had assets of $100 million or more, today there are in excess of 500 such concerns. This growth has enabled many concerns to accomplish what only a few were once capable of doing. The Du Pont company's experience illustrates well that enormous size is not a prerequisite of successful invention and innovation.

For over four decades Du Pont has been in the forefront of American industry in research and development. It has long had a more inventive and innovative spirit than other "large" chemical companies. It introduced moistureproof cellophane, duco-lacquers, Freon refrigerants in the 1920s, and neoprene and nylon in the 1930s. It is significant that Du Pont initiated its fundamental research program and made some of its most spectacular inventions and innovations in the 1920s, when it was only one-sixth its present size.

In sum, the alleged advantages of large-scale invention have been greatly exaggerated, and while in many industries the innovative process may require companies of rather substantial absolute size, this fact alone does not appear to dictate high levels of concentration. The large size and the rapid growth of the American economy have enabled most industries to support a relatively large number of companies of substantial absolute size. And mere size does not necessarily confer market power on large companies. As will be seen in Chapter 6, there are great differences in the performance of highly concentrated industries and that of moderately concentrated industries.

LARGE-SCALE PROMOTION AND DISTRIBUTION

It has been seen that economies of scale in production, research, and innovation do not dictate high levels of concentration in most industries. In many consumer goods industries the advantages of large-scale sales promotion clearly redound to the benefit of large companies. These advantages stem from the high costs required to achieve successful product differentiation—or, as the businessman expresses it, to achieve a "consumer franchise."

The most effective medium in advertising—network TV broadcasting, for example—is costly. Nationwide programing of a single TV series may run into millions of dollars. Unless a company has very large sales and a national distribution system, it cannot use this medium with maximum efficiency. As a result, in many industries a few very large companies command virtually all advertising.

The food industry well illustrates the point. Food manufacturers spend more on advertising—about $1.5 billion annually —than any other industry. Although there are over 30,000 food manufacturers, the fifty-six largest do the bulk of total advertising conducted by food manufacturers in various media: network TV, 88 percent; magazines, 78 percent; spot TV, 63 percent; and newspapers, 56 percent.

In the preceding chapter it was pointed out that in the postwar years increases in concentration were most common in the consumer-oriented industries. There is persuasive evidence that advantages of large-scale promotion were largely responsible for these increases. A recent study made by John M. Blair shows a strong tendency for concentration to increase in those consumer goods industries in which network TV advertising is most important.

In thirty-six industries for which comparisons could be made[10] more than two-thirds experienced increases in concentration. Not only did the increases outnumber the decreases two to one, but many of the increases were substantial. In eighteen industries the share of business done by the four largest firms rose by more than 10 percentage points. Few other American industries experienced corresponding increases. Nor were the increases restricted to industries having low levels of

[10] These were all industries in which a minimum of $250,000 was spent in 1963 on network television gross time billing. Testimony by John M. Blair, before the Subcommittee on Antitrust and Monopoly (Washington, D.C.: United States Senate, September 12, 1966).

concentration to begin with. In the following five industries where concentration was already at record highs at the beginning of the period, the top four companies greatly expanded their shares over the period: hard-surface floorings, 80 to 87 percent; cereal preparations, 79 to 86 percent; chewing gum, 70 to 90 percent; home freezers, 63 to 82 percent; and household refrigerators, 62 to 76 percent.

The amount spent on advertising by leading companies has grown to enormous proportions. In 1963 the top three automobile companies spent a total of over $70 million on TV advertising; American Motors spent $2.5 million, which was one-fourth of General Motors' expenditure on a single TV program, "Bonanza." In 1967 the country's top advertiser, the Procter & Gamble Company, spent $280 million in all forms of advertising.

There were some exceptions to the above trends. But in most of the consumer goods industries experiencing declining concentration, the declines appear to be due to special circumstances, which offset the concentration-inducing effects of large-scale advertising. (For example, frozen fruits and vegetables were highly concentrated in the immediate postwar years because the industry was new. Much of the subsequent decline occurred as additional products were added to this industry.) Importantly, however, in all but one of the eleven industries experiencing declines (where the share held by the top four declined), the fifth through the eighth largest firms either maintained or expanded their market share. This indicates that the erosion in the market share of top companies did not benefit small companies but mainly a second tier of large companies. In cigarettes, for example, where the share of the top four companies fell from 90 percent to 80 percent, the second tier of four companies increased their position from 9 percent to 20 percent. This development reflects the success of the second tier of companies in promoting filter-tip cigarettes, especially during the "tar derby" of the 1950s. Their success, too, was accompanied by a tremendous growth in advertising outlays.

In some industries the advantages of large-scale promotion are so enormous that only the very top concerns are big enough to reap the full advantages. Consider the frozen fruit and vegetable industry, where advertising outlays generally run in excess of 5 percent of sales on branded products.

According to a Federal Trade Commission (FTC) study, in 1962 the two industry leaders combined—General Foods and Minute Maid (now owned by the Coca-Cola Company)—spent $9.8 million on advertising, which was nearly as much as the combined outlay of 268 other companies. Although the third to the fifth largest companies—Libby, McNeill and Libby, Stokely-Van Camp, and Seabrook Farms—made average outlays equal to 8 percent of sales, their absolute expenditures fell far short of those of the industry leaders. This meant that while these companies had higher per unit advertising costs, they were not getting the same amount of coverage. The result? Not only were they at a cost disadvantage, but they failed to achieve the same degree of consumer acceptance for their brands. Both factors cut into profits. Whereas the two leaders enjoyed profits equal to 5 percent of sales, the profits of the next three companies averaged only 0.6 percent of sales. The FTC report observed on this point: "Advertising expenditures for the two leaders were only slightly higher than their before-tax profits, but the other three leaders spent nine times as much on advertising as they received in profits." [11]

Advertising and related promotion expenses are not the only sources of product differentiations that are so costly as to preclude all but large companies from success. In some industries the high costs associated with designing new styles, packages, and products, in addition to the high expense involved in introducing them, can create even greater scale advantages. The automobile industry is the leading example.

The automobile is a large, complex consumer item which holds many and frequent opportunities for real or superficial

[11] Staff report to the FTC, *Economic Inquiry into Food Marketing, Part II; The Frozen Fruit, Juice and Vegetable Industry* (Washington, D.C.: Federal Trade Commission, December 1962), p. 109.

changes in design and styling. In no other consumer item has "conspicuous consumption" reached such massive proportions. Each year consumers spend over $40 billion in the purchase and maintenance of their automobiles. This sum is greater than the gross national products of all but about eight nations of the world.

The chief form of competition among automobile companies is frequent model changes. In a recent study it was found that in 1961 retailing costs attributable to model changes cost the industry $679 million.[12] Changing the model of a single line of cars can cost in excess of $100 million. Quite clearly this amount alone could consume the resources of all but the very largest enterprise. When this expense is coupled with the high cost of year-in, year-out advertising expenditures—GM spent $173 million in 1965—it is not surprising that no successful entry has occurred in the United States automobile industry for decades. On the contrary, there has been a continued exodus of companies. At the end of World War II the industry consisted of the "big three" and a fringe of six small companies, each with from 1 percent to 5 percent of the market. Today the fringe has shrunk to one, and its prospect for successful survival is not good.

NET IMPACT OF SCALE REQUIREMENTS

In sum, what conclusion can be reached concerning the net effect of the economic causes of concentration discussed above? Most importantly, the imperatives of modern technology are not working toward monopoly. Recent empirical findings have shown no scientific basis for the Marxian, Schumpeterian, and related theories, which argue that "monopoly capitalism" is an inevitable result of modern technology. Reviewing the picture

12 F. M. Fisher, Zvi Griliches, and Carl Kaysen, "The Cost of Automobile Model Changes since 1949," *Journal of Political Economy* (October 1962).

broadly, the requirements of large-scale production are becoming a less important, not a more important, cause of industrial concentration. Nor do economies of large scale in research and innovation make high-level concentration inevitable in most industries, and they certainly do not explain the areas in which concentration increased most in the postwar years.

In contrast to the above two developments, advantages of large-scale promotion and distribution are clearly working toward increasing concentration. The postwar experience leaves little doubt on this matter. It was noted in Chapter 3 that the only broad industry groups experiencing more increases in concentration than decreases were in the consumer goods area, particularly those where advertising-achieved product differentiation is important. Other industries, on balance, experienced a significant net decline.

The best available empirical evidence does not support the thesis that modern technological imperatives make growing concentration either inevitable or necessary. Surprisingly, concentration has been increasing most in consumer goods manufacturing industries, which have relatively unsophisticated technology and in which private research expenditures are quite modest. In contrast, there has been a downward trend in producer goods manufacturing industries, which generally have larger production, capital, and R&D requirements than do consumer goods industries.

It is true that modern technology rules out highly fragmented industries consisting of vast numbers of companies. But only the unsophisticated will infer that the alternative to atomistic competition is monopoly. As will be seen below, the behavior of variously structured oligopolies differs widely. There is a broad spectrum of effective competition between fragmented industries and those approaching monopoly. Careful study of American industrial behavior reveals that most industries fall in this intermediate territory.

It should be emphasized that the factors discussed above are not the only ones determining the future structure of the economy. Or, put differently, merely because basic technological and economic forces do not require monopoly this is no guarantee that competition will endure or will emerge where it does not now exist. Suppose, for example, that the only barrier to new entry in an industry is the requirement that the output of an efficient plant is equal to 5 percent of the market. This would permit twenty efficient-sized plants to coexist in the industry. But there is no reason why the top four companies would hold no more than 20 percent of industry output. For example, a company would find it advantageous to acquire or consolidate with one or more other companies. There are no "natural" economic forces to prevent this. A series of mergers could quickly bring four-firm concentration to well over 50 percent. Another possibility is that while today the industry is large enough to sustain twenty efficient-sized plants, earlier in its history it could support only a few.

Or perhaps a monopoly initially was based on patents. But irrespective of the original cause for existing high levels of concentration, there is no reason to expect this high concentration to wither away merely because it is no longer required for efficiency reasons. In this case potential entry will place an upper limit on prices; however, potential competition is not always a good substitute for actual competition. There is no guarantee that "natural" economic forces alone will either preserve competitively structured industries or erode highly concentrated ones. Mergers and other forms of business conduct may more than offset underlying forces promoting competitively structured industry. Therefore the legal institutions governing business conduct may play a powerful role in either encouraging or deterring industrial concentration. Because mergers often play an especially crucial role in bringing about structural change, the next chapter deals specifically with this subject. But first a word about the way market concentration may be affected by the rate at which industries grow.

ECONOMIC GROWTH AND CONCENTRATION

When industrial concentration is high, it may be eroded by the entry of new companies. New entry is difficult, however, if there are significant economies of scale. For example, if a new entrant must achieve 10 percent of industry sales before it can operate efficiently, it most likely must incur heavy losses in an attempt to capture this much of the market. New entry is especially difficult if existing concerns already have excess capacity. Similarly, new entry would be expected to be most difficult in stagnant or slow-growing industries. On the other hand, when existing firms operate near capacity and industry sales are expanding rapidly, a new entrant may expect to share in a growing market, and therefore would not have to take much business away from existing enterprises.

Postwar concentration trends bear out these expectations. Although there were mixed trends in concentration, industry growth rates played an important conditioning role. As shown in Table 4.1, industries whose sales grew by less than 25 percent between 1947 and 1966 experienced an average increase in concentration of 2.9 percentage points. At the other extreme, industries whose sales grew by 300 percent or more experienced an average *decrease* in concentration of 3.3 percentage points.

Again, although the pattern between producer goods industries and consumer goods industries differed, concentration patterns in each group were related to industry growth rates. In producer goods industries, concentration decreased most in the rapidly growing industries; in consumer goods, concentration rose most in the slowest growing industries.

The relation between industry growth rates and industry structure has important implications for public policy. It suggests that rapid economic growth promotes effective competition. But while rapid economic growth may play an important

TABLE 4.1 / COMPARISON OF INDUSTRY GROWTH AND
CHANGES IN INDUSTRY CONCENTRATION

	AVERAGE CHANGE IN FOUR-FIRM CONCENTRATION		
Industry Sales Growth 1947–1966 (percent)	All Manufacturing Industries (percentage point change)	Producer Goods Industries (percentage point change)	Consumer Goods Industries (percentage point change)
Under 25	2.9	−0.3	7.9
25–149	1.8	−1.1	4.3
150–299	0.8	−0.7	5.3
300 and over	−3.3	−5.1	0.9
Average	0.7	−1.7	4.8

SOURCE: "Industrial Structure and Competition Policy," in *Studies by the Staff of the Cabinet Committee on Price Stability* (January 1969), p. 62.

role in eroding industrial concentration, business prosperity also unleashes powerful forces conducive to mergers, some of which may increase industrial concentration, the subject of the following chapter.

CHAPTER 5

Mergers and Industrial Organization

Mergers, more than any single economics factor, explain the existing structure of the industrial sector of the United States economy. Most contemporary big businesses owe their relative size to merger-accelerated growth, and current levels of concentration in many industries are directly linked to one or more of the merger movements that have swept through American industry.

Mergers are important in the study of industrial structure, because they represent a special kind of company growth. When a concern grows by expanding its own capacity and sales —developing and introducing new products—or by building its way into a new industry, such growth is subjected to the critical test of the market place. Simply put, a company must prove that there is a demand for *its* products or services—a harsh test indeed. It is ordinarily assumed, therefore, that when a company pursuing the *internal* growth route expands at the expense of its competitors, it has passed the test of the market place—has bested its rivals in a fair fight. In truth, so long as it uses "fair" methods of competition—it does not use predatory tactics and the like—it may even achieve a monopoly without being condemned. However, it is significant that there are few enduring examples of such internally achieved monopoly.

The "market test" of growth does not apply equally when a company grows by the merger route, that is, by acquiring or consolidating with another company. No market safeguard can ordinarily prevent one competitor from achieving monopoly control by consolidating with his leading rivals. In fact, the reverse is true. Many businessmen might willingly trade the vagaries of a competitive existence for the quiet life of monopoly. Hence, when oligopoly or monopoly is achieved largely by merger, there is no objective market test of whether the end product is deserved or not.

Industrial history provides many examples of how mergers have rapidly transformed an entire industry, leaving an indelible imprint for decades. Hence, the role played by mergers in bringing about structural change deserves special attention in the study of industrial organization and public policy. This chapter reviews the impact of three merger movements on American industry. Chapter 9 deals with public policy toward growth by merger. But first a word about the motives underlying growth by merger.

REASONS FOR COMPANY MERGERS

Economists have identified a number of reasons why companies often choose to grow by mergers. It must be recognized that a concern is motivated to merge for two reasons: desire for growth and factors that may make merger a preferred method of growth.

Ultimately, companies grow because their owners or managers wish to grow. It is important to recognize that human beings allocate resources, not the market place. This distinction is significant, because the introduction of human motivation and aspiration makes the growth process much more complex than is suggested by the economists' model that explains the growth of companies as an inevitable response to the spur of profit maximization.

Companies may wish to grow for a variety of reasons: to achieve economies of large-scale production or distribution, to attain market power, or simply to grow larger because doing so increases the absolute size and the overall prestige of the company and its management. One recent study strongly supports the hypothesis that large merging companies tend to be more oriented to managers' interests than to the profit maximization interests of stockholders.[1]

Whenever a company has any of the above incentives for growth, it next must decide on the most effective (from its standpoint) way of growing: internal expansion or merger. For many reasons, merger often seems the most desirable method of growth. It is quicker; it permits the purchase of personnel, products and know-how; it may be easier to finance; and, perhaps most importantly, it permits expansion of the company's position in an existing industry or entry into a new one without disturbing the competitive situation by adding new capacity and a new competitor to the industry. Because these factors favoring mergers are always present, companies with an incentive to grow (for whatever reason) will often find it to their advantage to grow by merger rather than by internal growth. But why then do mergers occur in cycles instead of being evenly distributed over time?

The rate of merger activity appears to be rather closely associated with overall business activity, or the so-called business cycle. This is to say, merger activity is positively correlated with good times in the business community. For example, the merger movement in the 1920s was choked off by the depression following 1929, and the first cycle of the current movement ended with the recession of 1948–1949. On the other

---

[1] John Bossons, Kolman J. Cohen, and Samuel Richardson Reid, "Mergers for Whom—Managers or Stockholders?" *Working Paper 14* (Pittsburgh: Carnegie Institute of Technology, April 1966).

hand, the 13 percent increase in industrial production and the 33 percent increase in industrial stock prices between 1954 and 1955 were associated with a rapid rise in merger activity. Mergers continued at a high rate into 1956 as industrial production rose another 4 percent. But with the slackening of business activity in 1957 and 1958, total merger activity fell off slightly. It revived once again with the expansion of 1959, fell off in 1960, and subsequently rose with business expansion.

Although there are many unique reasons underlying particular mergers, business prosperity and conditions in the stock market seem to create an economic environment which, when viewed from the vantage point of individual business enterprises, makes growth by merger especially attractive. Simply put, businessmen often view mergers as the cheapest and most profitable way of growing. In recent years merger promoters have discovered and employed an amazing array of financial and tax gimmicks that create the illusion of growing profits. This does not mean that particular mergers are inevitable or that companies will not grow if they cannot grow by merger. On the contrary, most growth in our economy is achieved by the internal growth route.

But while the precise causes underlying merger cycles may not be understood, industrial history does teach that business prosperity and intensive merger activity go hand in hand. As a Federal Trade Commission study on the subject observed in 1948: "Traditionally, this profits-merger spiral has been checked only by an economic collapse or by the virtual elimination of effective competition." [2]

THE GREAT MERGER MOVEMENT

Students of industrial organization generally agree that there have been three rather distinct merger movements. The first merger movement occurred around the turn of the century and

[2] *Report of the Federal Trade Commission on the Merger Movement* (Washington, D.C.: Federal Trade Commission, 1948), p. 20.

left a permanent imprint on the structure of American manufacturing. For the seven-year period, 1897–1903, 2,864 mergers were recorded.[3] Measured against the economy of 1900, the great merger movement was massive in its effects. By 1909, when the movement was about spent, and prior to the breakup of the petroleum, tobacco, and explosive trusts, the one hundred largest industrial corporations controlled about 17.7 percent of the assets of all industrial corporations.

This merger movement left many great corporations in its wake. United States Steel was organized in 1901 with the consolidation of eleven companies, some of which themselves were creatures of consolidation. Standard Oil of New Jersey was the other great "trust" of the day. United States Steel and Standard Oil (N.J.) used the merger route to become the world's two greatest corporations by 1909.

Many other of the big businesses of today had their genesis in the early merger movement. By 1905, E. I. du Pont de Nemours and Company absorbed over one hundred companies and emerged with a near monopoly of the explosives business. U. S. Rubber was created in 1893 through the acquisition of nine leading rubber companies. Additional mergers created the American Tobacco Company (1890), American Sugar Refining Company (1891), Diamond Match Company (1889), International Paper Company (1898), National Biscuit Company (1898), United Shoe Machinery Corporation (1899), American Can Company (1901), Amalgamated Copper Company (1901), and International Harvester Company (1902).

The great merger movement came to an end in 1903. Although the sharp stock market decline in 1903–1904 was the immediate occasion for terminating the movement, a contributing factor was that the merger promoters had pretty well exhausted the field of promising merger candidates.

During the next two decades mergers continued at a slow pace. But it was during this relatively quiescent period that today's largest manufacturing corporation was born and nur-

[3] Ralph L. Nelson, *Merger Movements in American Industry, 1895–1956* (Princeton, N.J.: Princeton University Press, 1959), p. 37.

tured by a succession of combinations and mergers. Following the merger in 1908 of the Buick Motor Company, Oldsmobile Motor Company, and Steward Body Company, the General Motors Company acquired over seventy-five additional automobile and related companies. Included were such familiar names as Cadillac, Chevrolet, Fisher, AC Spark Plug, and Champion Ignition, in addition to many others whose names were familiar to the automobile buyer of the 1920s. By 1929 General Motors had assets of $1.3 billion and was outranked by only United States Steel and Standard Oil (N.J.). Moreover, the General Motors Corporation had become linked to Du Pont, the world's largest chemical company, which had acquired a controlling interest in GM by the early 1920s.

THE SECOND MERGER MOVEMENT

The second merger movement started in the mid-1920s and reached what Willard L. Thorp described as the "hysteria stage" during the late 1920s. In the six-year period, 1925–1930, 4,682 mergers were recorded. At the peak of the movement, in 1929, 1,245 mergers occurred.

The merger movement of the 1920s transformed fewer industries than did its predecessor. The chief exception was the food industry, much of which had been left untouched by the earlier movement. National Dairy Products, created by a consolidation of dairies in 1923, acquired over 300 companies during the next eight years. These acquisitions, which included many well-established concerns, among them Kraft Cheese Corporation, propelled National into forty-first place in all manufacturing and third among food manufacturers. During the same period, the Borden Company greatly accelerated its growth by acquiring over 200 concerns. As a result of about twenty acquisitions, General Foods Corporation emerged as the first great conglomerate food manufacturer. Among its acquisitions are such well-known brands as Maxwell House,

Sanka, Jello, Birds Eye, Baker's Chocolate, and Swans Down Cake Flour. Other large food companies created mainly by the merger movement of the 1920s were General Mills, Continental Baking, Ward Baking, Beatrice Foods, and Purity Baking Company.

In contrast to the first merger movement, the second was not restricted to the industrial sector of the economy. Mergers played a big role in restructuring retail food distribution. In the decade ending with 1930, the seven leading retail food chains of that day acquired over 5,000 stores. These mergers greatly expanded the size and the geographic scope of operations of these companies. Each company, with the exception of A&P, owes much of its relative size to the mergers which it made in the 1920s. (These companies and their respective ranks in 1930 and 1968 were A&P, first and first; Kroger, second and third; Safeway, third and second; American Stores, fourth and fifth; First National Stores, fifth and tenth; National Tea, sixth and fourth; Grand Union, seventh and ninth. The change in ranks of these companies between 1930 and 1968 largely reflects the extent to which they grew by mergers subsequent to 1930.)

The first two merger movements established the main contours of many industries as they are known today. In the main, the same "big three" or "big four" companies still occupy the top positions in such basic industries as steel, automobiles, petroleum, tires, and copper, as they did when the second merger movement was choked off by the Great Depression.

Fully seventy-five of the one hundred largest industrial corporations of 1929 owed most of their relative size to mergers. Most of these companies, excepting those which themselves were subsequently acquired, are still among the top enterprises of today.[4]

[4] George W. Stocking, *Business Concentration and Price Policy* (New York: National Industrial Conference Board, 1955), p. 200.

THE CURRENT MERGER MOVEMENT

Merger activity paralleled the precipitous drop in industrial activity in the 1930s and did not revive until the latter years of World War II, when the third merger movement got under way. The trends in the current merger movement are depicted in Figure 5.1. The upper section shows the *trend* based on "total" mergers in manufacturing and mining.[5] The middle and the lower sections show the trend in "large" mergers for the period 1948–1968. The large acquisitions series includes only those companies whose assets at the time they were acquired amounted to $10 million or more. This large merger series is shown in terms of both the number of companies acquired (middle section) and the aggregate assets of the acquired firms (lower section).

The current merger movement has occurred in two rather distinct phases or cycles. The first took place during the period 1943–1947 and had an especially pronounced impact on the structure of particular industries, for instance, textiles and distilling.[6] For example, between 1940 and 1947, Schenley Distillers acquired thirteen distillers; Seagrams acquired eleven distillers; and National Distillers Products acquired six distillers.

Following 1947, merger activity subsided, reaching a postwar low in 1949. Thereafter it accelerated, rising sharply during the 1954–1955 surge in stock prices. Except for the recession of 1957–1958, the trend continued generally upward. In each year from 1958 to 1968, more than 800 manufacturing and mining mergers were recorded. Mergers reached frenzied levels in 1967 and 1968, when 1,500 and 2,400 mergers were recorded.[7]

[5] This total figure is based on mergers reported in *Standard Corporation Records* and *Moody's Industrial Manual*. Although these sources understate "total" merger activity, they accurately indicate the trend of merger activity.

[6] *Report of the Federal Trade Commission on the Merger Movement* (Washington, D. C.: Federal Trade Commission, 1948).

[7] See Appendix Tables A1 and A2 for a further breakdown of the mergers occurring since 1948.

Figure 5.1 / *Manufacturing and Mining Firms Acquired 1948–1968*

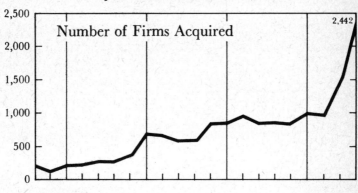

Number of Firms Acquired

2,442

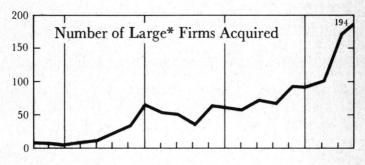

Number of Large* Firms Acquired

194

($ BILLIONS)

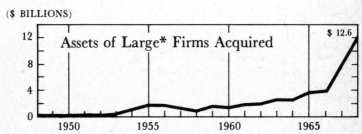

Assets of Large* Firms Acquired

$ 12.6

* Firms with assets of \$10 million or more.

SOURCE: Bureau of Economics, Federal Trade Commission.

The large merger series for the period 1949–1968 parallels the general upward movement displayed by the total merger series—in terms of both numbers and aggregate assets acquired. In the late 1940s and early 1950s acquired assets were well below $1 billion annually (Figure 5.1, lower section). Beginning in 1954 the assets moved over the $1 billion mark and have tended generally upward except during the recession years 1957–1958. In 1968 they reached an all-time high, when a total of 201 large mergers with combined assets of $12.8 billion were consummated—a 500 percent rise in acquired assets over the peak year level of the 1950s. In truth, the assets acquired in 1968 were as great as those acquired in the thirteen-year period, 1948–1960.

The current merger movement, like the movement of the 1920s, involves many segments of distribution as well as manufacturing. The number of mergers in services and trades has risen more rapidly in recent years than has that of industrial mergers. For example, since 1950, food retailers with combined sales of over $5 billion have been acquired.

Quite clearly, the United States is in the midst of an enormous merger movement. This is especially apparent when merger activity involving "large" industrial concerns is placed in perspective. As shown in Chapter 3, in 1969 the approximately 2,500 manufacturing companies with assets of $10 million or more controlled 86 percent of the assets and 88 percent of the profits of all manufacturing corporations. Consequently mergers among companies in this size group are especially important.

During the period 1948–1968, 1,206 manufacturing companies with assets of $10 million or more were acquired. Just how significant these large mergers have been in terms of the total number and the assets of all large manufacturing companies is shown in Table 5.1. The table compares the number and the assets of acquired companies falling in various size classes with the total number of such companies in 1968.

These comparisons reveal that the 697 acquired companies

TABLE 5.1 / NUMBER OF ACQUISITIONS AND MANUFACTURING ASSETS ACQUIRED, 1948–1968, COMPARED WITH TOTAL MANUFACTURING, 1968

	NUMBER		
Size Class of Acquired Firm (millions)	Companies Acquired 1948–1968	Total Companies 1968*	Acquisition as Percent of Total 1968
$ 10–$ 25	701	1,117	63
$ 25–$ 50	274	507	54
$ 50–$100	138	284	49
$100–$250	71	257	28
$250 and over	22	272	8
Total	1,206	2,437	49
	ASSETS		
	Total Assets Acquired 1948–1968 (billions)	Total Manufacturing Assets 1968* (millions)	Acquisition as Percent of Total 1968
$ 10–$ 25	$10.5	$ 18.0	58
$ 25–$ 50	$ 9.6	$ 18.3	52
$ 50–$100	$ 9.4	$ 20.8	45
$100–$250	$ 9.9	$ 39.4	25
$250 and over	$10.3	$287.4	4
Total	$49.7	$383.9	13

* First quarter

SOURCE: Federal Trade Commission, *Staff Report on Corporate Mergers,* 1969.

with assets between $10 million and $25 million were equal to 63 percent of the total number, and 58 percent of the total assets, of all companies of this size operating in 1968. At the other extreme, twenty-two companies with assets of over $250 million were acquired, representing 8 percent of all companies of this size in 1968.

In short, merger activity took a heavy toll among companies with assets in excess of $10 million, particularly those with assets between $10 million and $100 million. If these companies had not been acquired and if they had continued in business,[8] at least[9] an additional 50 percent of companies with assets of $10 million or more would have been operating in 1968 than were actually operating.

Most of these acquisitions were made by the country's largest industrial corporations. During 1948–1968, the 200 largest companies alone accounted for well over one-half of all acquired assets of large companies (Appendix Table A2).

Acquisitions by 200 Largest Corporations

Between 1948 and 1968 the 200 largest manufacturing corporations of 1968 made at least 3,864 acquisitions with combined assets of $50 billion (see Table 5.2).[10] This number represents a truly enormous volume of resources. It is greater than the total value of the assets held by all manufacturing corporations in 1900. Put another way, between 1948 and 1968 these 200 concerns absorbed assets 94 percent as great as those they had held in 1948.

All size groups among the top 200 made a substantial vol-

8 Very few of these companies were failing concerns.

9 An unknown, though probably quite large, number of companies would have entered the $10 million size class had they not been acquired. During 1948–1968, over 1,100 companies in the $5–10 million asset class were acquired. Had these companies not been acquired, many would doubtless have grown into the $10 million and over class.

10 Asset information was not available for 903 of these acquisitions. Most of these presumably were small companies. As shown in Appendix Table A2, during 1966 and 1967 the top 200 companies acquired seventy-two companies (each with assets of $10 million or more) with combined assets of $5.7 billion. They also acquired an undetermined number of companies with assets of less than $10 million.

TABLE 5.2 / ACQUISITIONS BY 200 LARGEST MANUFACTURING
CORPORATIONS, 1948–1968

Size of Acquiring Corporation*	Number of Acquisitions	Total Assets Acquired (millions)	ACQUIRED ASSETS AS PERCENT OF	
			1948 Assets	1968 Assets
5 largest	65	$ 1,293	13	2
6–10	42	$ 675	10	2
11–20	141	$ 4,483	60	13
21–50	512	$11,975	115	20
51–100	1,182	$13,334	148	23
101–150	1,019	$13,478	222	40
151–200	894	$ 4,765	135	21
Total	3,864	$50,003	94	17

* Companies ranked by total assets in 1968.

SOURCE: Federal Trade Commission, *Staff Report on Corporate Mergers*, 1969.

ume of acquisitions. Companies ranking among the top five acquired a large volume of assets—about $260 million each. But since the top five were so much larger than the others to begin with, these acquisitions represent a *relatively* small part of their current size. Acquisitions were equal to 13 percent of the size of the top five companies in 1948 and 2.3 percent of their size in 1968 (Table 5.2). Mergers were much more important to other companies ranking among the top 200, particularly those ranking below the fifty largest. The acquired assets of companies ranking fifty-first to two hundredth were equal to over 20 percent of their assets in 1968. This figure represents a minimum estimate of the contribution of mergers to the growth of these companies, since it takes into account only the *direct* contribution of mergers to their growth. (Mergers have an *indirect* as well as a direct effect on growth. Although the immediate effect of an acquisition is to increase the size of the acquiring company by an amount equal to the size of the acquired company, most mergers also make a continuing contribution to the growth of the acquiring company.)

The country's 200 largest industrial corporations have been active acquirers throughout the course of the current merger movement. As shown in Appendix Table A2, during the period of 1948–1968, acquisitions by the top 200 accounted for nearly half of the number of "large" acquired companies and over 60 percent of the assets of these companies.

The merger pace of the top 200 has quickened in recent years. In fact they acquired twice as many assets during the 1960s as during the preceding twelve years.

COMPETITIVE RELATIONS OF
MERGING COMPANIES

A key issue in appraising the competitive effect of a merger is the market relationship between the acquired companies and the acquiring companies. Earlier merger movements—particularly the great merger movement around 1900—were characterized by combinations among direct competitors. Not so the current movement.

It is conventional to classify mergers into three broad categories: horizontal, vertical, and conglomerate. Conglomerate mergers in turn may be further placed in three subcategories: geographic market extension, product extension, and "other."

Horizontal mergers are those in which the merging companies produce one or more closely related products in the same geographic market, for example, two fluid-milk companies in the city of Chicago. *Vertical* mergers are those in which the merging companies have a buyer-seller relationship prior to merger, for example, an aluminum ingot manufacturer and an aluminum product fabricator. *Conglomerate* mergers of the *geographic market extension* type are those in which the acquired and the acquiring companies manufacture the same products but sell them in different geographic markets, for example, a fluid-milk distributor in New York and a fluid-milk distributor in Chicago. Conglomerate mergers of the *product extension* variety are those in which the acquired and the acquiring companies are functionally related in production and/ or distribution but sell products that do not compete directly with one another—a merger between a soap manufacturer and a bleach manufacturer. Pure *conglomerate* mergers involve the union of two companies that do not have any buyer-seller relationships, nor are they functionally related in manufacturing or distribution—a shipbuilder and an ice cream manufacturer.

When mergers are subdivided in accordance with the above classifications, a marked change in the relative importance of various types of mergers may be seen (Table 5.3). On the one hand, the relative volume of horizontal mergers declined substantially—from nearly 40 percent during 1948–1951 to about 4 percent in 1968. On the other hand, the percent of conglomerate type mergers increased from 37 percent in 1948–1951 to 89 percent in 1968. The sharp reduction in horizontal mergers has been caused in part by antitrust enforcement policy, which challenged a high percentage of large horizontal mergers occurring since 1950 (see Chapter 9).

TABLE 5.3 / PERCENT OF ACQUIRED ASSETS, BY TYPE, 1948–1951 AND 1968

| | PERIOD | |
| | 1948–1951 | 1968 |
Type of Merger	(percent of total)	(percent of total)
Horizontal	39	4
Vertical	24	7
Conglomerate	37	89

SOURCE: Federal Trade Commission, *Staff Report on Corporate Mergers,* 1969.

The current merger movement, especially in the last few years, has been essentially conglomerate. Typically, mergers occur between companies operating in different economic markets or, in the language of the economist, between companies selling products that have low cross elasticities of demand. This is not to say the merging companies have nothing in common; on the contrary, they frequently have related technologies or distribution systems.

Many large mergers, however, are between companies that appear to be entirely unrelated. For example, the International Telegraph & Telephone Company (IT&T) is a huge international conglomerate operating over 150 affiliated companies in fifty-seven countries; it is the fourth largest private industrial employer in the world. Most of its present size can be traced to the hundreds of mergers it has made during the years. During 1961–1968 it acquired at least 120 businesses with combined assets of nearly $2 billion. Perhaps more than any other corporation, ITT has acquired companies that are themselves large and leaders in their fields. For example, it has acquired Avis, the second largest car rental corporation; Sheraton Corporation, the largest hotel chain; Continental Baking Company, the country's largest bakery products manufacturer; and Educational Services, one of the leading suppliers of educational exhibit materials. During the first nine months of 1969, ITT's board of directors approved the consumation of thirty-three more acquisitions. Three of these were industry leaders with combined assets of about $2.2 billion: Grinnel Corporation, the nation's leading maker of automatic fire protection equipment, Canteen Corporation, one of the largest vending machine companies, and Hartford Fire Insurance Company, a leader in several lines of insurance. (The government has challenged each of these mergers under the antimerger act.)

Other examples of recent conglomerate mergers were the takeover of RKO theatres and Schenley Industries by Glen Alden, a diversified company in textiles and other fields; the acquisition of the Yankees baseball team by CBS; the absorption of Sunshine Biscuit Company by American Tobacco; the merging of Continental Oil and Consolidated Coal; the purchase of Mack Trucks by Signal Oil; the acquisition of Peabody Coal by Kennecott Copper; and the purchase of Container Corporation of America by Montgomery Ward.

The implications of growing industrial conglomeration are explored separately in Chapter 6. But insofar as the conglomerate enterprise poses economic and other problems, the current merger movement is their wellspring. The expanding share of total manufacturing done by the top 200 concerns provides a rough index of the growing conglomeration of big business. As noted in Chapter 3, between 1947 and 1968 the share of total manufacturing assets held by the 200 largest industrial concerns rose from 47.2 percent to 60.9 percent, and the share held by the one hundred largest grew from 40.1 percent to 49.3 percent. Hence by 1968 the share held by the one hundred largest firms was greater than the share held by the 200 largest in 1947.

The increases in concentration reflect in part the influence of the extensive merger movement under way since the mid-1950s. Over the period 1948–1968 the 200 largest manufacturing firms alone acquired over 3,000 concerns with combined assets exceeding $50 billion. Most of the increased share of total industrial assets held by the top 200 firms is attributable to these numerous mergers.

Theoretically, a merger may injure, enhance, or neutralize competition. But more is required than mere speculation. The precise fashion in which the current merger movement has affected the competitive performance of the economy requires detailed analysis of particular mergers. Such analysis requires knowledge of a merger's impact on industry structure: does it increase industry concentration, raise barriers to entry, or involve the elimination of significant potential competitors?

Although no comprehensive analysis has been made of the competitive effects of the current merger movement, this much is clear: Unlike past merger movements, horizontal mergers have *not* restructured many industries. Early in the current merger movement the government successfully challenged mergers between important direct competitors—the so-called horizontal mergers (Chapter 9). For example, the government's challenge in 1956 of the proposed merger of the Bethlehem and the Youngstown steel companies clearly had a strong impact on the structure of the steel industry. When the court sustained the government's position, leading steel companies as well as leaders in other industries recognized that they could not buy up competitors. This policy has doubtless been an important factor in molding the postwar structure of the steel industry, which experienced a modest decline in market concentration between 1954 and 1963. (Between 1954 and 1963 the top four companies' share of total shipments of blast furnaces and steel mills fell from 55 percent to 50 percent. The proposed Bethlehem-Youngstown merger alone would have been sufficient to offset this decline in concentration. In 1954 Bethlehem had 16 percent of industry capacity, and Youngstown had 5 percent.) Had it not been for the stringent public policy toward horizontal mergers, many industries would doubtless have experienced sharp increases in concentration. In fact, public policy toward horizontal mergers—that is, mergers between direct competitors—had pretty well eliminated such mergers by leading companies by the early 1960s.

Just as horizontal mergers by industry leaders have reached a historic low, conglomerate mergers reached an all-time high in 1968. While the competitive effects of such mergers are less obvious, under certain circumstances they too may lessen competition. (Chapter 6 contains a discussion of the conglomerate enterprise and the way in which some conglomerate mergers have injured competition.) Although all may not agree on the probable consequences of such mergers, they clearly are bringing about sharp increases in aggregate concentration in the economy. Industrial history argues persuasively that prosperity unleashes powerful economic forces conducive to mergers. It is therefore safe to predict that so long as prosperity continues, public policy will be the most crucial factor determining the future direction and magnitude of conglomerate mergers and, ultimately, the organization of much of the American economy.

CHAPTER 6

Market Power in Action

INTRODUCTION

The essence of the distinction between competition and monopoly is the absence or the presence of market power. It was stated in Chapter 2 that economic theory teaches that certain characteristics of a market's "structure" confer economic power on its inhabitants. Most importantly, market power gives a company some *discretion* in making pricing and output decisions.

But economic power is not merely a theoretical construction. It is an observable and a measurable phenomenon. When firms have discretionary power over prices and other decisions, they are likely to use it. Judge Learned Hand put it well when he said that the monopolist "must sell at some price and the only price at which it could sell is a price which it itself fixed. Thereafter the *power and its exercise must needs coalesce.*" [1]

Hence concerns with substantial market power may be expected to behave differently from those with moderate or little power.

1 *United States* v. *Aluminum Co. of America,* 148 F. 2d 416 (1945). [Emphasis added.]

This chapter and the next one deal with the use and the consequences of market power. This chapter probes briefly the business practices and policies of concerns with market power: how they price, destroy or weaken rivals, restrain new entry, and garner to themselves large profits. The next chapter analyzes how market power may frustrate monetary and fiscal policy designed to maintain full employment and to stimulate economic growth.

PRICING POLICIES

Only in atomistic markets with numerous sellers behaving independently are all sellers price takers. In such markets sellers have no pricing policies; the market determines prices. But when sellers are few, there invariably is an area of discretion, at least in the short run, within which they may set or "administer" their prices. Economists therefore often use the terms "oligopoly pricing" and "administered pricing" interchangeably.

But administered pricing covers a multitude of sins. The most relevant question is not whether *some* discretion over price exists, but how much and how it is exercised and whether it is good or bad for the economy. As noted earlier, economic theory predicts that the market conduct of sellers is largely determined, or at least conditioned, by market structure. But, importantly, a given structural setting may give sellers discretion to pursue any number of market strategies. Consequently, the ultimate performance of an industry (for example, the size of its profits) depends upon the particular strategy employed. Only a few of the variety of policies that may have an impact on the ultimate performance of an industry will be identified here.

Collusion and Cartels

It has been seen that economic theory predicts that oligopolists will price interdependently rather than independently. But interdependent pricing does not necessarily result in a monopoly price, provided formal collusion does not exist. Indeed, the best proof of this is the great length to which oligopolists will go, if permitted to do so, to replace tacit agreement with formal collusion. Collusive pricing may take a variety of forms. The most extreme variety involves elaborate agreements for fixing prices, dividing markets, allocating customers, and even pooling total receipts. Collusive arrangements embracing a number of restraints on trade are generally called cartels. Some early American cartels even included elaborate procedures for penalizing members for breaking the agreement. Because it is difficult to keep secret the details of elaborate cartel arrangements, cartels are rarely found today in domestic American markets. Most contemporary collusion takes the form of attempts to fix prices, and such collusion is relatively short-lived.

One of the most important recent instances of price fixing involved the "great electrical conspiracy." In 1960 twenty electrical manufacturers and forty-five of their executives were indicted on charges of price fixing, bid rigging, and market sharing in the sale of a wide assortment of products ranging from turbine generators to circuit breakers. In 1961 General Electric, Westinghouse, Allis Chalmers, and other electrical equipment manufacturers pleaded guilty to the conspiracy.

This conspiracy maintained prices at artificially high levels. After the conspiracy was discontinued, prices on some items fell by as much as 50 percent.[2]

The consumer may pay dearly when prices are fixed at artificially high levels. For example, in 1965 the leading wholesale bakers and the largest food chain in the state of Washington

---

2 Ronald Wolf, "Identical Pricing and TVA," in *The Economic Impact of TVA* (Knoxville, Tenn.: University of Tennessee Press, 1967), p. 93.

were found guilty of having suppressed price competition and of having maintained uniform and noncompetitive prices in most of the major cities in the state.[3] The conspiracy extended back to at least 1955.

In this case it is possible to estimate the cost of the conspiracy to consumers in the state. Prior to the conspiracy, bread prices in Seattle, Washington, were about equal to the United States average. On the other hand, during most of the eleven-year period 1954–1964, Seattle prices averaged between 15 percent and 20 percent above the United States average. After the competitors were found guilty in 1964 of violating the antitrust laws, Seattle bread prices dropped sharply, and today they are slightly below the national average.

If it is assumed that residents of the state of Washington consumed about the same amount of bread as other Americans,[4] between 1954 and 1964 Washington consumers each year paid about $3.5 million more than they would have paid had their prices been equal to the national average, or about $35 million over the entire period. If all American consumers had been paying these higher prices for bread during this period, they would have spent about $3 billion more for bread than they actually did.

Price behavior in the sale of broad-spectrum antibiotic drugs provides another illustration of the high cost of price conspiracy to consumers. In 1967 a New York District Court found five drug companies—American Cyanamid, Charles Pfizer, Bristol-Myers, Upjohn, and E. R. Squibb—guilty of fixing prices of this drug, beginning in 1951. Over the ten-year period, 1952–1961, wholesale prices of broad-spectrum antibiotic drugs were $5.10 per bottle of sixteen tablets. Because manu-

[3] Federal Trade Commission, *Economic Report on the Baking Industry* (Washington, D.C.: Federal Trade Commission, November 1967), p. 68.

[4] The demand for bread is very price-inelastic; i.e., the amount consumed does not vary greatly with changes in price. The national average bread consumption is fifty-three pounds a person. With a 3- to 4-cent inflated price and with an affected population of nearly two million people, this equals roughly $3 million to $4 million each year.

facturing costs averaged well below 50 cents per bottle, this price enabled the drug makers to reap tremendous profits. Consumers paid hundreds of millions of dollars more for this drug than they would have had prices been at competitive levels. After these companies were indicted in 1961, prices dropped sharply, until by 1967 they were two-thirds below the price existing during the conspiracy. After the parties were found guilty many states and municipalities brought suits for damages suffered by the conspiracy. In 1968 the five drug companies offered to pay damages totaling $210 million. At this writing, the matter has not been settled.

It is no exaggeration to say that if cartels and price conspiracies were permitted to flourish in the American economy, consumers would pay literally billions of dollars more each year for their purchases. Not only do cartels result in higher prices; they almost invariably also result in higher costs and decreased efficiency. First, cartel prices are frequently set to cover the cost of the least efficient member; second, when price competition is eliminated, companies often resort to various forms of expensive nonprice competition which inflate their costs. For example, Seattle bakers engaged in the conspiracy discussed above had much greater per unit distribution costs than did bakers in other cities. This illustrates the well established fact that companies engaged in cartel arrangements do not necessarily enjoy large profits, because cartels encourage, or at least permit, high cost operations.

Attempts to fix prices are probably commonplace in many industries. This practice poses the most serious economic problem in highly concentrated industries. Although businesses in less concentrated industries also have a strong *incentive* to collude, their efforts in this respect often prove short-lived. When sellers are numerous, it is difficult to make prices stick without an elaborate cartellike arrangement. Because such arrangements are easy to detect and are illegal, they seldom are resorted to today. Hence, collusive pricing most often is a serious problem in highly concentrated industries, where fewness of sellers makes it less necessary to engage in elaborate price-fixing procedures. Here, a word to the wise may be sufficient to create a perfect understanding.

Price Leadership

Sellers in many concentrated industries recognize one of their own as the industry price leader. Usually the leading firm is chosen, or chooses, to act as the price maker or price leader for the industry.

This practice should surprise no one. After all, oligopolists have a pricing problem. Because there are only a few sellers, each seller recognizes that his pricing actions will have an impact on those of his rivals. How then shall prices be set? Demand and cost conditions change over time. Hence, prices must also be changed from time to time. But when and by how much? These are questions about which even friends may disagree. Because outright collusion is illegal, oligopolists most often find that the best solution is to put their faith in the pricing decisions of the industry's leading firm.

For decades United States Steel was its industry's acknowledged price leader. In its early years its famous "Gary dinners" served as the forum for United States Steel's expressions of price policy. These meetings served to educate the lesser industry members—apparently with considerable success. As United States Steel President Judge Gary put it in 1907, "We have secured as a rule the maintenance of fair prices; we have avoided injuring our neighbors who are in competition with us." After these dinners ended in 1911, United States Steel remained the industry price leader for decades.

Other companies that have at one time or another been acknowledged price leaders are International Harvester, in agricultural machinery; Standard Oil (N.J.), in petroleum; and the Great Atlantic and Pacific Tea Company, in food retailing. In truth, the industrious student is likely to identify some company as the price leader in nearly every oligopolistic industry.

What, then, is the significance of this phenomenon? Students of the steel industry are generally agreed that United States Steel's price leadership policy played a key role in stifling competition in the steel industry. But it is wrong to equate all price leadership with monopoly pricing. All price leaders do not have the same degree of discretion in "making" prices. Economists have identified a spectrum of situations. At one extreme, the price leader can set a monopoly price. At the other extreme, the price leader is little more than a price barometer and cannot price significantly above competitive levels.

Close analysis shows that the exact position of an industry between these extremes depends mainly on the key structural elements of market concentration and the barriers to entry. Where there are many sellers, the price leader who sets prices well above competitive levels soon finds them eroded, because some rivals make secret price concessions. Examples are many canned fruits and vegetables and fresh meat products. Even if there are only a few sellers, a price leader will be reluctant to set prices far above competitive levels if doing so encourages a rash of new concerns to enter the industry. On the other hand, where there are few sellers and high entry barriers, the price leader may set prices that yield a monopoly return. The cigarette industry fits into this category, as did the steel industry until recent years, when international competition placed a limit on the domestic price that can be charged for many steel products.

Hence, the identification of a price leader is only the beginning of an analysis of monopoly power. One must examine other elements of any industry's structure and behavior to determine the monopoly power wielded by a price leader. When the price leader is supported by formal collusion among competitors, monopoly pricing almost surely will result. Similarly, when an industry's sales are concentrated in only a few hands, a price leader is able to set monopoly prices. But importantly, the real culprit is the structure of the industry, not price leadership as such. Thus the monopoly problem cannot be solved by merely telling one company not to lead or other companies not to follow.

Predatory and Discriminatory Practices

Companies that already enjoy a degree of market power may entrench or enhance their positions through various anticompetitive practices. They may engage in tactics that intimidate, coerce, destroy, or forestall the entry of weaker competitors. Such *predatory* practices include selling at ruinously low prices, cutting off a competitor's source of supply, or foreclosing distribution outlets by long-term supply contracts or tying arrangements.

Such practices were common instruments of the trusts around the turn of the century. The classic examples of its use are to be found in the creation of the tobacco, petroleum, and powder trusts. For example, in the latter part of the nineteenth century the leading explosives manufacturers engaged in predatory price campaigns to destroy or weaken their rivals. The most common practice was first to weaken a competitor by selling at disastrously low prices in its markets and then to acquire it. As a result of its numerous predatory price campaigns and its nearly one hundred acquisitions, by 1909 E. I. du Pont de Nemours and Company achieved a virtual monopoly over much of the explosives business.[5]

Following passage of the Sherman Act in 1890 and the Clayton Act in 1914 (Chapter 9), the most brazen predatory practices pretty well disappeared from the American business scene, although more subtle kinds of anticompetitive conduct continued. Most important among these are various kinds of discriminatory conduct.

[5] As a result of these actions, in 1912 Du Pont was found guilty of having violated the Sherman Act and was forced to divest itself of about one-half of its explosives business. *United States* v. *E. I. du Pont de Nemours and Co.*, 188 Fed. 127 (1912).

Price discrimination refers to the practice of selling to different customers at prices that do not reflect cost differences. Price discrimination may occur in selling (1) to different customers, (2) to different geographic markets, and (3) different products.

Customer discrimination occurs when a seller grants its big buyers favored treatment over small buyers, even though the costs are the same for each group of customers. For example, powerful buyers may sometimes be able to extract discriminatory prices from their suppliers, with the result that the competitors of large buyers may be seriously injured. An illustration of this practice is the discriminatory price discounts granted by the Morton Salt Company to its largest customers. Prior to a 1948 Supreme Court decision, Morton had the following price discount schedule:

	Per Case
Less-than-carload purchases	$1.60
Carload purchases	1.50
5,000-case purchases in any consecutive 12 months	1.40
50,000-case purchases in any consecutive 12 months	1.35

Only the country's five largest food chains—A&P, Safeway, Kroger, American Stores, and National Tea—purchased in sufficient quantities to enjoy the maximum discount. Consequently retailers buying in less-than-carload lots paid 18 percent more, and those buying in carload lots paid 11 percent more, than did the five largest chains.

At first blush this arrangement might not seem to have placed other retailers at a significantly competitive disadvantage, since salt is only one of many products sold by food stores. If, however, large buyers are permitted to extract significant price concessions on many of their products, they would soon have an enormous advantage over smaller concerns. This is particularly true in food retailing, where customary pretax profit margins average about 2.5 percent of sales. The Supreme Court recognized this probability in its decision finding the above discriminatory price schedule in violation of the Robinson-Patman Act. The court concluded, "Since a grocery store consists of many comparatively small articles, there is no possible way effectively to protect the grocer from discriminatory prices except by applying the prohibitions of the Act to each individual article in the store." [6]

Geographic price discrimination occurs when a seller charges different prices in different locations. Around 1900 the Standard Oil trust used this practice to destroy or intimidate competitive oil companies in different sections of the country. In recent years this practice has been used by some large fluid-milk-processing concerns to destroy local competitors.

Product discrimination occurs when a seller charges different prices for essentially identical products—in terms of cost and quality. The low-priced product may be used as a "fighting" brand to weaken competitors, thereby enhancing the market for the "premium" brand.

Price discrimination in favor of large buyers would be commonplace were it not for the antitrust laws. For example, between July 1, 1954, and July 30, 1965, the country's nine largest corporate food chains were recipients of unlawful discriminatory prices in sixteen separate antitrust cases.[7]

The above are only the chief variants of discriminatory pricing. Not all price discrimination is anticompetitive. The competitive effects of discrimination depend on the size and other characteristics of those practicing it and those affected by it. Under a special set of circumstances, price discrimination may actually enhance competition. The argument is sometimes made that when a highly concentrated industry sells to big buyers (for example, cigarette companies to large food chains), a big buyer's demands for price favoritism may erode an otherwise rigid price structure. But the validity of this argument rests on the assumption that the discriminatory prices are temporary and that all buyers soon pay the same prices. If big buyers persistently receive special price concessions, this situ-

---

[6] *Federal Trade Commission* v. *Morton Salt,* 334 U.S. 337 (1948).

[7] Federal Trade Commission, *Staff Report on Food Retailing* (Washington, D. C.: Federal Trade Commission, 1966), p. 183.

ation tends to transform the structure of the buying industry. As a result, persistent price discrimination is therefore more likely to beget monopoly than competition.

Reciprocal Selling

When sellers are few and price competition is muted, companies frequently turn to various kinds of nonprice competition. In certain industrial markets oligopolists resort to reciprocal selling—the practice of "I'll buy from you if you'll buy from me."

A certain amount of reciprocal selling comes quite naturally in all human intercourse. Even the clergyman is likely to patronize the shops of his flock.

But under certain conditions reciprocity can have an important impact on competition—(1) where a firm's potential customers are its potential suppliers, and (2) where some concerns in an industry can employ the practice more extensively than can others. Both conditions usually are related to the relative size and conglomeration of the companies in an industry. If all companies in an industry produce only a single product and are of the same size, none could use reciprocity to gain an edge over his rivals.

But suppose, for example, that one explosives manufacturer is a large, conglomerated enterprise, whereas all others are specialized explosives manufacturers. The large size and conglomeration of this one manufacturer would doubtless make it a much larger potential purchaser of products made by its potential explosives customers. The reader might question whether any explosives manufacturer could employ the practice. After all, who buys explosives and also sells to explosives makers? Such buying and selling may require multilateral reciprocal trade arrangements. A 1935 incident involving the Du Pont Chemical Company is a classic illustration of multilateral reciprocity.

A director of Atlas Powder Company, Du Pont's second largest explosives rival, wrote the following letter to the president of Du Pont, which not only was the largest explosives company —as well as the world's largest chemical company—but also controlled the General Motors Corporation. The Atlas director explained that Du Pont

> [was seeking to] get a bigger share of the explosives business of the Rochester and Pittsburgh Coal Company . . . [which] sells largely to the Castonia Paper Company, which in turn is owned largely by the Curtis Publishing Company. . . . Du Pont [sic] put the pressure on the Curtis Publishing Company, based on their own and (by inference) General Motors' advertising account, to have the coal company increase its purchases of explosives from them.[8]

Not too surprisingly, the Rochester and Pittsburgh Coal Company began purchasing explosives from Du Pont.

Fortunately for Atlas, it was able to work out an arrangement whereby it agreed to purchase all its trucks from Chrysler in return for Chrysler's promise to apply pressure on the Curtis Publishing Company. This counterattack enabled Atlas to keep about 49 percent of the business. If Atlas had been a small, specialized explosives company, it would have been helpless in blunting the Du Pont attack.

Opportunities for business reciprocity have risen as more concerns are becoming increasingly conglomerated. A recent study showed that 100 percent of the purchasing agents surveyed reported that reciprocity is a major factor in buyer-seller relations in the chemical, petroleum, and steel industries.[9] Over three-fourths of these buyers said that they divided purchases on a reciprocal basis.

A leading chemical company explained the success of its reciprocity program as follows:

[8] Quoted in George W. Stocking and Willard F. Mueller, "Business Reciprocity and the Size of Firms," *Journal of Business* (University of Chicago, April 1957), p. 84.

[9] Leonard Sloane, "Reciprocity: Where Does the P.A. Stand?" *Purchasing*, November 20, 1961, p. 70.

Sales to our 100 largest suppliers were $29,414,000, an increase of $7,032,000. The $7,032,000 represents sales to new customers who are suppliers. It also represents increased sales to old customers with whom sales ties are stronger now as a result of our trade relations activities.[10]

The records in a recent antitrust case illustrate the manner in which reciprocity is practiced today. According to Judge John M. Cannella, the General Dynamics Corporation made extensive use of reciprocal selling during 1958–1962.[11]

In 1957 the General Dynamics Corporation acquired the Liquid Carbonic Corporation. Prior to the merger, General Dynamics made the great bulk of its sales to the United States government. This prevented it from using its purchasing power to further sales. By acquiring Liquid Carbonic, General Dynamics was able to bring its purchasing power to bear on suppliers who now purchased a product made by General Dynamics.

General Dynamics established an elaborate reciprocity operation to insure the effective use of its overall purchasing power in furthering its sales. A senior vice-president candidly stated that the purpose of the program was "to aid the Liquid Carbonic sales picture via General Dynamics' reciprocity leverage." The officer in charge of reciprocity put it equally bluntly: "Let's not kid ourselves, the ultimate reason for establishing a trade relations department is to increase sales through the proper application of your purchasing power." [12] The record of this case illustrates that General Dynamics was not "kidding itself." It used its reciprocity power in the hope of gaining sales, and its hopes were realized.

When reciprocity becomes widespread in an industry, it not only dulls price rivalry among existing competitors but also makes it difficult for new firms to enter the industry. A potential competitor will find that much of the market is foreclosed

10 *Ibid.*, p. 74.
11 *U.S.* v. *General Dynamics Corporation,* U.S. District Court, Southern District of N.Y., August 26, 1966.
12 *Ibid.*

to him. This may act as a formidable entry barrier for even large, powerful potential entrants.

All reciprocal selling is not equally injurious to competition. But the best that can be said for reciprocity is that sometimes it may have no significant adverse competitive effects. As the Supreme Court has observed, however, "The practice results in an irrelevant and alien factor, intruding into the choice among competing products, creating at the least a priority on the business at equal prices." [13]

MONOPOLY POWER AND EXCESS
PROFITS

Direct evidence of the manner in which market power raises prices and curbs output is difficult to come by. The best single indication of how market power distorts the economic process is seen in the level of profits in competitive and noncompetitive industries.

Profits play a central role in allocating resources in a market economy. The prospect of profits or the fear of losses translates the forces of supply and demand into operating decisions of a concern. When competitive pressures are keen, industry profits adjust toward the cost of capital. Such adjustment occurs because as long as prices result in profits above the cost of capital, additional capital is invested. When market concentration is high and there are substantial barriers to new entry, prices can be set at levels insuring profits far above the cost of capital.

Relative profit levels, therefore, serve as a good indicator or "proxy" of the degree of discretionary pricing power and the resulting misallocation of resources.

Several recent studies illustrate the close association between market concentration and level of profits. Table 6.1 classifies eighty-five large food manufacturing companies according to

[13] *Federal Trade Commission* v. *Consolidated Foods Corporation*, 380 U.S. 592 (1965).

TABLE 6.1 / RELATIONSHIP BETWEEN INDUSTRY CONCENTRATION AND PROFITS IN FOOD MANUFACTURING

Industry Concentration (percentage of share held by top four companies)	Number of Companies	Net Profit on Stockholder Equity (percentage)
31–40	21	6.2
41–49	32	9.2
50–59	15	12.9
60–69	6	14.6
70–90	11	16.3
Total	85	10.4

SOURCE: Federal Trade Commission, *Staff Report on Food Manufacturing* (Washintgon, D.C.: Federal Trade Commission, June 1966), p. 204.

the average level of concentration of the industries in which they operate.[14] For example, twenty-one companies operated in industries where the top four companies did less than 40 percent of the business—industries such as meat packing and canned fruits and vegetables. These companies earned an average after-tax profit of 6.2 percent on their invested capital. Obviously they were earning profits quite close to the "cost" of capital. At the other extreme, eleven companies operated in industries where the top four companies controlled 70 percent or more of the business—industries such as breakfast cereals and canned soups. These companies enjoyed an average profit rate of 16.3 percent, or about two and one-half times greater than those companies operating in the least concentrated group of industries. Between these two extremes, profits tended to rise as concentration rose. It appears that in industries where the top four companies controlled 50 percent or more of sales, companies were able to earn returns well above the cost of capital. Significantly, well over one-half (62 percent) of the

---

[14] Because most companies operated in more than one industry, each company was classified according to the weighted-average level of concentration of the industries in which it operated.

eighty-five companies studied operated primarily in industries with concentration ratios below 50 percent.[15] At the other extreme, only seventeen (20 percent) operated primarily in industries with concentration ratios of 60 percent or more. (These companies accounted for only 12 percent of the sales of all eighty-five companies.) This indicates that most large food manufacturing companies operate in the middle and lower ends of the oligopoly spectrum; that is, their performance approximates the competitive norm more closely than the monopoly norm.[16]

Other studies also show that profit rates exceed competitive levels when industry concentration is high.[17] As would be expected, on the basis of economic theory, profits depart most from competitive levels when both concentration and entry barriers are very high. In this situation oligopolists may charge high prices without fearing that new entrants will be attracted to their industry. One study shows that, although all highly concentrated industries tend to enjoy noncompetitive profits, industries with high entry barriers enjoyed the highest profits. Of twenty-one highly concentrated industries (in each industry, eight companies held over 70 percent of sales), the eight judged to be most difficult to enter had average profits 50 percent higher than the other highly concentrated industries.[18] This confirms the expectation that resource allocation is most distorted where both concentration and industry barriers are high.

Industries with these characteristics include automobiles,

[15] *Op. cit.,* p. 206. The eighty-five companies included in Table 6.1 did about one-half the business of all food manufacturers.

[16] Another study of food manufacturers, although using different techniques, comes to conclusions similar to those shown in Table 6.1. Norman R. Collins and Lee E. Preston, "Concentration and Price Margins in Food Manufacturing Industries," *Journal of Industrial Economics* (July 1966), pp. 226–242.

[17] Joe S. Bain, *Barriers to New Competition* (Cambridge, Mass.: Harvard University Press, 1956).

[18] H. Michael Mann, "Seller Concentration, Barriers to Entry, and Rates of Return in Thirty Industries, 1950–1960," *Review of Economics and Statistics* (August 1966), p. 300.

ethical drugs, cigarettes, sulfur, nickel, and flat glass. The leading firms in each industry earned average net profits in excess of 15 percent on invested capital over the eleven-year period 1950–1960, and in some years, well in excess of 20 percent.

Sellers of these products often face some competition from substitute products. But the persistently large profits of high-concentration, difficult-to-enter industries bear eloquent proof that interproduct competition is an inadequate substitute for effective competition from sellers of the same products. In many products, the potentially most powerful restraining force on excessive prices and profits is import competition. Free international trade has the effect of reducing seller concentration.[19] For example, during the 1960s growing international competition brought keen pressures to bear on certain steel products.

It was noted in Chapter 2 that advertising and promotion could create substantial entry barriers and thereby elevate profits. A recent econometric study uncovered a significant positive correlation between advertising intensity and profits of an industry. After adjusting statistically for other factors that may affect profits, such as differing industry growth rates, it was found that industries with high advertising outlays enjoy profits about 50 percent greater than those industries with low advertising outlays.[20]

Concerns with market power do not always reap high profits. Under some circumstances concerns with market power may charge excessive prices without earning high profits. A prominent example is steel pricing during much of the 1950s. In that period the industry had a large volume of excess capacity. Had competition been effective, steel prices would have been pushed down. Instead, however, the steel industry used its power to maintain prices well above competitive levels, and actually raised prices in 1958 in the face of declining demand.

[19] See, in this series, Jan Pen, *A Primer on International Trade* (New York: Random House, 1967).

[20] William S. Comanor and Thomas A. Wilson, "Advertising, Market Structure, and Performance," *Review of Economics and Statistics* (November 1967), pp. 423–444.

As a result, the industry was able to operate profitably—although at moderate profit levels—with as much as 50 percent of its capacity idle. This instance is an elegant demonstration of the possession and use of market power. In Chapter 8 it will be shown that authoritative studies estimate that the oligopolistic pricing behavior of the steel industry played a significant role in the price inflation occurring between 1954 and 1960 and in the deterioration in the balance of payments in the years that followed.

CONGLOMERATE-DERIVED POWER
AND ITS USE

Traditional theories of monopoly and oligopoly deal with the behavior of companies operating in particular industries or markets. But these theories are inadequate in explaining the competitive tactics available to companies operating across many markets. This defect in these theories becomes more and more important as an increasing number of large enterprises become conglomerated.

The conglomerate enterprise has many more tools in its competitive kit than does the specialized business. Because it operates across many markets, its potential customers are often also its potential suppliers, and it is thus able to engage in reciprocal selling, as discussed above. The more conglomerated a company becomes in relation to its rivals, the greater are its reciprocity opportunities.

When the conglomerated enterprise enjoys market power in some markets or industries, it may use its monopoly profits to subsidize its expansion elsewhere. In these and other ways market power held in one industry may be used as a vehicle for achieving power elsewhere.

The key to the unique advantage enjoyed by the conglomerate enterprise is that it operates across many markets, either separate "product" markets or separate "geographic" markets. For example, large retail food chains may achieve conglomerate power when they operate in many cities, in some of which they hold strong market positions. The large retail food chain referred to in Table 6.2 enjoyed substantially higher profits in

TABLE 6.2 / MARKET SHARE AND NET PROFITS OF A LARGE FOOD CHAIN IN 304 CITIES

Share of Sales (percentage)	Number of Cities	Contribution to Warehouse Profits* (cents per dollar of sales)
4.9 and under	25	0.2
5.0– 9.9	68	2.1
10.0–14.9	70	4.3
15.0–19.9	41	4.9
20.0–24.9	40	5.9
25.0–34.9	34	6.0
35.0 and over	26	6.9

* These are the profits at the retail level exclusive of warehouse overhead expenses.
SOURCE: Federal Trade Commission, *Staff Report on Food Retailing* (Washington, D.C.: Federal Trade Commission, 1966), p. 89.

those cities where it had a large share of the business than it did in cities where it held a small share. These differences are especially important, because pretax profits of food retailers average only about 2.5 cents per dollar of sales. This chain used the profits of its highly profitable markets to subsidize its expansion into new markets. For example, in one area it incurred losses of $2.4 million during 1955–1959 while expanding its sales by 140 percent—from $11.2 million to $26.7 million.[21] Nor was this an isolated experience. The record further discloses that this chain was able to sustain high profits over a period of years in markets where it already had achieved strong market positions. Moreover, in such markets it generally had higher gross profit margins, which measure the difference between selling prices and cost of goods sold.

[21] *Ibid.*, pp. 106–111.

Apart from using conglomerate power to subsidize expansion, the conglomerate may also use such power to destroy, weaken, or discipline competitors. For example, during the 1950s one large retail food store chain engaged in deep and widespread price cuts in certain of its markets where it faced strong competition. Safeway Stores, Incorporated, the country's second largest retail food store chain, had sales of $3.3 billion in 1966 and operated food stores in twenty-seven states, as well as in Canada, England, West Germany, and Australia. It ranks as one of the top four retailers in three-fourths of the metropolitan areas in which it operates. Because of its multimarket characteristics and the strong position it holds in some markets, Safeway has the capacity to concentrate large resources in particular markets.

Between 1954 and 1955 Safeway used these resources to engage in an especially intense price war in its Dallas and El Paso, Texas, divisions.[22] Over a sixty-four-week period the depth of its price cuts grew, and the number of items sold below invoice costs rose sharply, reaching a peak of nearly one-fourth of the 2,000 items in the grocery departments checked by the Federal Bureau of Investigation. In one price zone below-cost items were 17.1 percent below invoice costs.

Despite the severity of Safeway's losses in these divisions over a fifteen-month period—allegedly amounting to $4 million—its total company profits were not seriously affected. In 1954 Safeway enjoyed profits of $29 million on its overall operation.[23]

The competitive tactics employed by the Proctor & Gamble Company provide another illustration of the possession and

22 *Ibid.*, pp. 121–141.
23 As a result of these actions the government charged Safeway with violations of Section 2 of the Sherman Act and Section 3 of the Robinson-Patman Act. *U.S.* v. *Safeway Stores, Inc., et al.*, Criminal No. 9484. This case was settled by a plea of *nolo contendere.* Substantial fines were imposed upon the defendants, and two Safeway officials were given suspended jail sentences. A companion civil action was settled by the signing and entering on December 7, 1967, of a consent decree, which placed restraints on Safeway's subsequent pricing behavior.

use of conglomerate power. In 1967 P & G had sales of $2,439 million and after-tax profits of $141 million. With advertising expenditures of $280 million it was the country's largest advertiser. P & G manufactures a wide range of household consumer items sold through grocery, drug, and department stores. It is especially big in household detergents, in which it accounts for over one-half of United States sales.

The record of a recent antitrust case provides a striking example of how P & G was able to achieve and retain positions of market dominance. In 1957 it introduced a household cleanser under the Comet brand. Over a twenty-two-month period it spent $7.2 million for advertising and sales promotion of this product. Twenty months after its introduction, Comet held 36.5 percent of the national market in abrasive cleansers. This was at an annual sales rate of about $19 million. Unquestionably, P & G could not have achieved this market position if it had not been a large conglomerate enterprise with vast resources available from other high-profit operations.

The record in this case also illustrates how P & G was able to ward off competitive thrusts of smaller enterprises. In 1957 Purex, the second largest household bleach company, with total sales of $50 million, launched a major attack on P & G's strong position in the Erie, Pennsylvania, market. (P & G held over 50 percent of the market at the time.) By marketing its liquid bleach in a new container and by means of cents-off labels and coupons, Purex won a share of over 30 percent of the market. P & G immediately counterattacked with strenuous promotional efforts coupled with intensive advertising expenditures, soon forcing Purex's share down to 7 percent of the market. A Purex officer testified that because of his company's inability to cope with P & G's "brand war," it decided to merge with a competitor.

Nor are these isolated examples. A small company, Adell Chemical, developed and introduced liquid detergents under the Lestoil brand.[24] In a short period of four years its share of

24 F. M. Scherer, Statement before the Select Committee on Small Business (Washington, D.C.: U.S. Senate, March 2, 1967).

sales was driven from nearly 100 percent to a bare 12 percent, after P & G and Lever Brothers introduced—with a tremendous push of promotion and advertising—brands competitive with Lestoil.

The above examples illustrate how conglomerate-derived power may be used. Such power is not an idle instrument. Judge Learned Hand's observation that monopoly "power and its exercise must needs coalesce" probably also applies to the inevitability of the use of conglomerate-derived power. To have it is to use it—unless restrained by public policy.

The discretionary power of the conglomerate enterprise may extend beyond purely economic decisions. Use of such discretion may have broad antisocial implications, according to a Department of Justice suit challenging the proposed acquisition of the American Broadcasting Company by the International Telegraph and Telephone Corporation. The Justice Department argued that IT&T, a huge international conglomerate embracing 150 affiliated companies in fifty-seven countries, might influence ABC's public affairs programing. Indeed, during the course of the trial, testimony was presented that IT&T attempted to manipulate the news coverage of the proposed merger by applying pressure on newsmen. The merger was subsequently abandoned.

A recent study by William G. Shepherd uncovered an interesting relationship between market power and another contemporary social problem—discrimination in employment. Shepherd found an inverse relation between the level of industry concentration and the relative number of Negroes employed.[25] In other words, the more competitively structured the industry, the higher the percentage of Negro employment among professional employees. These findings led Shepherd to conclude that "Generally speaking, it is in competitive firms and non-profit agencies that employment tends to be relatively non-discriminatory, not in firms with market power." The findings indicate that companies holding great discretionary

[25] "Market Power and Racial Discrimination in White Collar Employment," *Anti-trust Bulletin* (Spring 1969), p. 155.

power in making price and related decisions cannot be relied upon to use such power voluntarily in the public interest, whether judged by either social or economic criteria.

SUMMARY

The preceding examples illustrate some manifestations of market power. The reader should recognize that these are the exception, not the norm, of behavior of American business enterprise. The examples are drawn largely from the records of antitrust cases, and in this sense they resemble the experience of the doctor who, not too surprisingly, sees mainly the sick portion of the population. On the other hand, concerns with substantial power may sometimes exercise their power in ways so subtle that they cannot be observed easily and which do not violate existing antitrust statutes.

No longer is there reason to doubt that an industry's profits and prices are determined largely by various market structure variables, especially the degree of market concentration, the height of entry barriers, and the extent of product differentiation. Recent studies demonstrate, moreover, that profits approximate the competitive norm (i.e., they about equal the cost of capital plus a risk premium) when four-firm control is less than 40 percent of the market. This is an important empirical finding. It demonstrates that competition can be effective in oligopolistic market structures that fall between the polar extremes of single-firm monopoly and atomistic competition. While there are a number of industries where market concentration is too great to permit effective competition, the greater part of American industry is quite competitively structured. Fortunately, in relatively few industries do technological imperatives require very high market concentration. On balance, it is effective competition, not monopoly, that is the rule in American industry.

CHAPTER 7

Market Power, Price Stability, and Full Employment

INTRODUCTION

The Employment Act of 1946, a law based on the belief that mass unemployment is both intolerable and unnecessary, charged the federal government with the responsibility of maintaining maximum employment and rapid economic growth. The basic premise of the act is that government should employ monetary and fiscal policies to create an environment conducive to economic growth. The act further assumed, however, that the private sector of the economy would provide the driving force of growth, expressly declaring that the government's full-employment policy would be pursued "in a manner calculated to foster and promote free competitive enterprise and the public welfare."

The unparalleled economic growth record of the 1960s demonstrates the dynamic responsiveness of free competitive enterprise to growth opportunities in a buoyant economy. Gross national product increased from an annual rate of $472 billion in the first quarter of 1961 to $723 billion in the first quarter of 1969. (Both figures are expressed in 1958 dollars.) This increase of $251 billion exceeds the total GNP of $227 billion (also in 1958 dollars) in 1940. In other words, the growth of the American economy over the past eight years has exceeded its total growth during the more than 150-year period between 1776 and 1940. It cannot be emphasized too strongly, however, that whereas federal monetary and fiscal policy has been an effective force in creating an environment conducive to growth, the actual expansion itself was accomplished by the private sector of the economy—both labor and business—with a minimum of direct intervention and planning by government.

An in-depth analysis of the fiscal and monetary measures used to promote sustained prosperity without inflation, the subject matter of the "new economics," [1] is far beyond the scope of this book. A few words are in order, however, on the significance of competition to monetary and fiscal policy aimed at full employment.

MARKET POWER AND INFLATION

The great English economist John Maynard Keynes, father of the "new economics," provided a persuasive theory demonstrating that, because of inadequate demand, the economy could in fact stagnate at a low-level equilibrium, one with excessive unemployment. While Keynes recognized that the assumption that wages, prices, and profits are set in essentially perfectly competitive markets was not universally met in the real world, he believed the exceptions to it were relatively unimportant to his basic thesis. While agreeing that businesses and trade unions could have "considerable practical significance," he viewed them generally as "positions of semi-inflation" as contrasted "to the absolute inflation which ensues on

[1] Walter W. Heller, *New Dimensions of Political Economy* (New York: Norton, 1967).

an increase in effective demand in circumstances of full employment." [2]

Nor was Keynes particularly concerned with the misallocation of resources resulting from monopoly. His "complaint" against a free enterprise system was that too often it did not fully utilize its resources.[3]

It must be recalled that Keynes was writing in the mid-1930s and that he was concerned with putting people back to work. When 10 percent to 15 percent of the labor force is idle and a large part of the industrial machine is silent, getting the economy going again overshadows the misallocation problem. Similarly, when prices and profits are severely depressed, one is hardly haunted by the specter of inflation.

But priorities change once the industrial machine is humming again. Then the effectiveness of competition and allocative efficiency takes on major importance in "growth" economics. Alfred E. Kahn states well the key role that effective price competition plays in this intricate job of promoting economic growth:

> For if there is one point about the relationship of prices to growth on which I think most economists would agree, it is that one essential for economic progress in a private enterprise economy is the aggressive pursuit of price-reducing policies by its leading business firms.[4]

Economic growth can also be throttled by the measures required to fight price inflation—that is, by restrictive monetary and fiscal policies, even though too many men and machines are still idle.

There are two general types of inflation, "demand-pull" and

[2] *The General Theory of Employment, Interest and Money* (New York: Harcourt, Brace & World, 1936), pp. 301–302.

[3] *Ibid.*, pp. 378–379.

[4] "Public Policies Affecting Market Power," in *Administered Prices: A Compendium on Public Policy* (Washington, D.C.: U.S. Senate, Subcommittee on Antitrust and Monopoly, Committee on the Judiciary, 88th Cong., 1st Sess.), p. 168.

"seller-induced." In demand-pull inflation "too much money is chasing too few goods;" this is the kind of inflation that followed World War II and that can be dealt with only through a reduction in the demand for goods by a combination of monetary and fiscal policies. While these policies will not be discussed here,[5] it should be carefully noted that, in a perfectly competitive economy, inflation can occur only because of excess demand. But the world is not perfectly competitive.

When some sellers have market power, inflation is possible *even in the absence of excess demand*. This is seller-induced inflation. Business enterprises with great discretion in administering prices can, and on occasion do, raise prices even in the face of falling demand. In a dynamic economy demand increases in some industries and decreases in others. When market competition is working properly prices would ordinarily be expected to rise in industries with growing demands and to fall in industries with declining demands. Similarly, the rate of productivity advance is higher in some industries than in others. In a competitive economy, other things being the same, industries with above-average productivity gains would show price decreases and those with below-average productivity gains would show price increases. Overall price stability can only be achieved, of course, if the industries registering price increases are offset by those showing decreases. But business concerns with market power can distort the pricing process by maintaining—or even increasing—prices in the face of falling demand, or by failing to decrease prices when they enjoy above-average productivity gains.

Organized labor also may cause seller inflation if it is successful in demanding wage increases that exceed increases in productivity. This is usually called "cost-push" inflation, a pushing up of production costs by labor. While this kind of labor-originated cost-push inflation could theoretically occur in any industry with powerful labor unions, it most often

[5] See Robert L. Heilbroner and Peter L. Bernstein, *A Primer on Government Spending* (New York: Random House, 1963).

occurs in those industries in which strong labor unions bargain with concerns having substantial market power. First, the large profits of such firms entice labor to ask for a bigger piece of the pie. Second, labor believes that management of these concerns has sufficient pricing discretion to "pass on" higher wage costs to consumers. Moreover, because concerns with significant market power do in fact have the capacity to pass on wage increases, they are more likely to grant wage demands exceeding productivity increases than are the concerns that do not have this power. Research studies show that wage rate increases are indeed related to the level of industry profits.[6]

The price behavior of the steel industry during the 1950s illustrates how concerns with market power can contribute to seller inflation. By 1953 the wartime inflation had spent itself, and during 1953–1955 the wholesale price index remained stable. Thereafter it began to rise. Steel prices played a major role in these increases. Between 1953 and 1959 finished-steel prices rose by 36 percent, in contrast to an 8.5 percent increase for all wholesale prices. In fact, wholesale prices exclusive of those of metals and metals manufacturers were only 1.5 percent higher in 1959 than they had been in 1953. Quite clearly, then, steel provided the mainspring for the price increases during that period.

The persistent increases in steel prices during 1953–1959 cannot be explained simply by the theory of demand-pull inflation. Not only was demand *not* pulling up steel prices, but at times prices were *raised* in the face of *falling* demand and the presence of substantial excess capacity. For example, steel prices were increased in 1954 despite the fact that capacity utilization fell from 95 percent in 1953 to 71 percent in 1954. The 1958 increases, viewed in terms of the demand-pull theory, were especially perverse, with overall capacity utilization dropping from 85 percent in 1957 to 61 percent in 1958.

These sharp price increases resulted in a widening in steel

[6] George Perry, *Unemployment, Money Wage Rates, and Inflation* (Cambridge, Mass.: M.I.T. Press, 1966).

producers' margins after 1953. Gardiner Means' careful analysis shows that producer margins at a standard rate of production about doubled between 1953 and 1959.[7] His analysis reveals that steel prices rose much more rapidly than per unit operating expenses—36 percent versus 14 percent.

By increasing margins the industry was able to operate profitably at a very low rate of capacity utilization. For example, Means estimates that because of the widening profit margins, in 1959 United States Steel would have been able to break even at an operating rate of 30 percent of capacity. In fact, during the first six months of 1960, while operations were at only 47 percent of capacity, the company enjoyed a net income after taxes of $111 million.[8] In contrast, if it had maintained only the profit margin prevailing in 1953, it would not have made any income at this rate of capacity utilization.

Steel price inflation between 1953 and 1959 thus cannot be explained by the traditional theory of demand-pull inflation. Otto Eckstein and Gary Fromm conclude their detailed analysis of these price developments with the observation that "the wage and price behavior of the steel industry represents an important instance of inflation caused to a substantial degree by the exercise of market power. This type of inflation cannot be controlled by policies aimed at restricting total demand." [9]

What is the significance of seller-induced inflation of this kind? In the terms of technical economics, this results in a poor "Phillips curve." It is now generally recognized that a short-run relation exists between the rate at which resources (labor and capital) are utilized and the general level of prices. A Phillips curve, named after the British economist, A. W. Phillips, measures the "trade-off" between rate of unemployment and annual wage and price increases. That is to say, it measures

7 *Pricing Power and the Public Interest* (New York: Harper & Row, 1962), p. 137.

8 *Ibid.*, p. 148.

9 "Steel and the Postwar Inflation," Study Paper No. 2 (Washington, D.C.: Joint Economic Committee, 86th Cong., 1st Sess., November 6, 1959), p. 34.

how much price inflation must be "traded" for a specified reduction in the rate of unemployment.

The curves shown in Figure 7.1 provide two hypothetical
illustrations of this relation for a nation. For example, point *A*
on curve number 1 would yield an unemployment rate of 5
percent and an annual price increase of 1 percent. In contrast,
point *B* would yield an unemployment rate of 3 percent and
an annual price increase of 5 percent.

Figure 7.1 / *Hypothetical Phillips Curves of Nation*

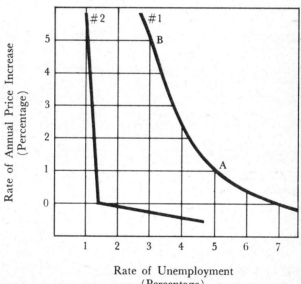

Obviously, it would be highly desirable if the Phillips curve
could be *shifted to the left*, thus improving the trade-off between unemployment and price inflation; that is, making it
possible to achieve a given level of unemployment with less
price inflation.

A number of factors determine the short-run shape and location of a country's Phillips curve. Theoretically, if a nation's prices were determined in perfectly competitive markets, its Phillips curve would look like curve number 2 in Figure 7.1. This would permit the country, in Paul A. Samuelson's words, to "engineer fiscal and monetary expansion just up to the point of full employment. Prior to that point, the general price level would not rise and average wages would grow automatically with productivity." [10] Samuelson adds: "In this ideal world, which differs dramatically from every mixed economy that now exists, the problem would be merely one of the macroeconomic dosage, and there would be no dilemmas of policy." [11] But, as shown in the above illustration of the steel industry, powerful unions and sellers can and do bring about seller-induced inflation. In this case, monetary and fiscal policies alone cannot be used to achieve full employment without inflation. Although monetary and fiscal policies can be used to "engineer" a desired point on a given Phillips curve, they cannot be used to manipulate the location of the curve itself. Hence, to do this—to improve the Phillips curve itself—other policies are needed, policies designed to supplement macroeconomic tools.[12] Here the discussion will be concerned with one of the main causes of a poor Phillips curve, namely, seller-induced inflation. (Other factors affecting the shape and the location of a country's Phillips curve include a variety of so-called structural problems in labor and capital markets.)[13]

[10] Arthur F. Burns and Paul A. Samuelson, *Full Employment, Guideposts and Economic Stability* (Washington, D.C.: American Enterprise Institute for Public Policy Research, 1967), pp. 53–54.

[11] *Ibid.*

[12] Even small improvements in a nation's Phillips curve may have an impact on national wealth. Shifting a Phillips curve to the left by 1 percentage point would enable a nation to pursue a monetary-fiscal policy that reduces unemployment by an additional 1 percent without an inflationary effect. At the employment levels of the early 1960s, reducing unemployment by 1 percent increased GNP by about $20 billion. Arthur M. Okun, "The Gap Between Actual and Potential Output," in *The Battle Against Unemployment* (New York: Norton, 1965).

[13] See "The Unemployment-Inflation Problem," Study Paper No. 4,

Since traditional monetary and fiscal policies are inadequate to deal with seller-induced inflation, what are the alternative methods of dealing with it? There are three: (1) formal price and wage controls, (2) an improvement in the competitive performance of the economy, or (3) some form of voluntary or semivoluntary restraints on prices and wages.

The United States has rejected the first alternative. Formal price controls represent an unacceptable solution except under the most pressing circumstances.

Although the second alternative holds much promise, it is only a partial solution. As will be seen, antitrust policy can have an important impact on the long-run structure and performance of the economy; but even under the most ideal circumstances, such policy would be impractical, particularly in the short run, to bring about sufficient industrial restructuring to eliminate all the problems created by seller-induced inflation.

The United States began experimenting with voluntary wage-price restraints in the early 1960s, a policy known as the "wage-price guideposts."

WAGE-PRICE GUIDEPOSTS

The President's Council of Economic Advisers first presented the guideposts in its January 1962 report to the President, explicitly recognizing that in some industries "private parties" had "considerable discretion" in determining wages and prices. As a result, the council concluded, "There is considerable room for the exercise of private power and a parallel need for the assumption of private responsibility." [14]

In essence, the council's "guideposts for noninflationary

Studies of the Cabinet Committee on Price Stability (January 1969), pp. 125–148.

[14] *Economic Report of the President* (Washington, D.C.: Council of Economic Advisers, January 1962), p. 185.

wage and price behavior" called for the kind of wages and prices generated by competitive markets. The report stated:

> The general guide for noninflationary wage behavior is that the rate of increase in wage rates (including fringe benefits) in each industry be equal to the trend rate of over-all productivity increase. General acceptance of this guide would maintain stability of labor cost per unit of output for the economy as a whole—though not of course for individual industries.
>
> The general guide for noninflationary price behavior calls for price reduction if the industry's rate of productivity increase exceeds the over-all rate—for this would mean declining unit labor costs; it calls for an appropriate increase in price if the opposite relationship prevails; and it calls for stable prices if the two rates of productivity increase are equal.[15]

The guideposts were not entirely novel. Earlier councils—and presidents—had called for labor and business restraint, but their admonitions had been general and imprecise. The 1962 report of the council made the problem quite explicit: Some companies and labor unions had great discretionary market power; unless that power was restrained, either inflation would be inevitable or it would be impossible to push on toward full employment.

Moreover, the guideposts achieved added stature when they were subsequently embraced as presidential policy. Walter W. Heller, chairman of the council at the time the guideposts were first announced, explains: "They had the President's blessing, but not, at first, a tight embrace. Increasingly under President Kennedy and fully under President Johnson they became Presidential policy." [16]

As first presented by the council, the guideposts, designed primarily to educate and mobilize public opinion, spelled out explicitly how wages and prices should behave if seller-induced

15 *Ibid.*, p. 189.
16 Heller, *op. cit.*, p. 43.

inflation was to be avoided. Thus, wages should be geared to productivity increases, which the council estimated to be 3.2 percent annually. And overall price stability also requires price reductions in those industries with high productivity so as to offset price increases in those with low productivity.

Quite clearly, then, the guideposts were directed at holders of market power, both strong labor unions and strong industrial firms. As Heller put it, they

> try to bring to the bargaining tables and board rooms where wage and price decisions are made a sense of the public interest in noninflationary wage and price behavior. Indeed, they try to appeal also to labor and management's broad self-interest in avoiding a self-defeating price-wage spiral.[17]

Kermit Gordon, also a member of the council in 1961 and 1962 and one of the principal architects of the guideposts, explains that their "focus was not on all wage and price decisions, but on the decisions of those groups which exercised important market power." [18]

Robert M. Solow sums up succinctly the logic underlying the guideposts:

> In an imperfect world, there are important areas where market power is sufficiently concentrated that price and wage decisions are made with a significant amount of discretion. When times are reasonably good, that discretion may be exercised in ways that contribute to premature inflation. . . . People and institutions with market power may, in our culture, be fairly sensitive to public opinion. To the extent that they are, an educated and mobilized public opinion may exert some restraining pressure to forestall or limit premature inflation.[19]

[17] *Ibid.*

[18] Joint Economic Committee of the Congress, *Twentieth Anniversary of the Employment Act of 1946: An Economic Symposium* (Washington, D.C.: Joint Economic Committee of the Congress, February 23, 1966), p. 63.

[19] "The Case Against the Case Against the Guideposts," in George P. Schultz and Robert Z. Aliber, *Guidelines, Informal Controls and the Market Place* (Chicago: University of Chicago Press, 1966), p. 44.

GUARDIANS OF THE GUIDEPOSTS

The 1962 Economic Report made no mention of the machinery to be used in "encouraging" compliance with the wage-price guideposts. It soon became apparent, however, that the council—often with the public support of the President—would become the guardian of the guideposts. It is not entirely clear whether the council had anticipated the role it was soon to play, or whether that role was thrust upon it by future events.

In any case, the first and greatest test to be faced by the guideposts occurred less than three months after they had been unveiled. Not too surprisingly, the industry involved was steel. As noted earlier, steel-pricing behavior had played a major role in the seller-induced inflation of the 1950s.

. In early April 1962, the steelworkers' union accepted a wage settlement calling for an increase in hourly wages of about 2.5 percent, a "noninflationary" settlement that fell well within the guideposts and which had been urged upon the union by the Kennedy administration.[20] The week following the settlement, United States Steel announced a general price increase of 3.5 percent. The next day, Bethlehem (the second largest steel producer) and five other companies followed suit with identical price increases, an action reminiscent of the behavior of the 1950s, since the industry was again operating well below two-thirds of capacity. These price increases represented a clearcut use of discretionary pricing power.

What followed is familiar history. President Kennedy announced that the price increases were in direct conflict with the wage-price guideposts, reminding the industry that the recent wage settlement could be offset by productivity increases and urging those steel companies that had not yet increased

---

[20] This discussion and the following one are based on John Sheahan, *The Wage-Price Guideposts,* (Washington, D.C.: Brookings, 1967), pp. 33 ff.

their prices—notably Inland, Armco, and Kaiser—not to follow United States Steel's lead. Shortly thereafter, Inland and Kaiser publicly announced that they would not follow the lead. Bethlehem—and shortly United States Steel—then withdrew their own price increases.

While the episode was all over in three days, bitter memories lingered. At first, much of the business community was highly critical of the episode. These emotional reactions soon subsided, however, and—perhaps most important—steel prices remained stable over the next four years. The wholesale index of steel and iron prices did not rise between the end of 1961 and the end of 1963, and by April 1966 the index was only 2 percent above the 1961 level.

This is not to say, however, that during this period the guideposts were always successful in restraining discretionary price increases.

For example, the council devoted special attention to the automobile industry in 1963–1964. As one of America's largest industries, the automobile industry is often a meaningful barometer of what occurs elsewhere in the economy. Moreover, it represents one of the most troublesome kinds of situations to be dealt with under the guideposts. Because the industry enjoys above-average productivity increases, its prices not only should not increase; they actually should decrease. To achieve this result would, of course, be no mean task in an industry with a powerful union and powerful manufacturers.

In its 1964 Annual Report, the council suggested that it would be particularly "appropriate to focus special attention this year on *price reductions . . .* in those industries whose trend productivity gains exceed the national trend," [21] adding the wry observation: "It is fair to say that large industrial enterprises thus far have not widely heeded this advice." [22]

During the year, the council argued that, in view of the au-

---

[21] *Annual Report of the Council of Economic Advisers* (Washington, D.C.: Council of Economic Advisers, January 1964), p. 120 [emphasis in original].

[22] *Ibid.*

tomobile industry's high profits and high productivity, prices could reasonably be lowered. The automobile union stated that it would keep its wage demands within the guideposts *if* the auto companies would first cut prices. After reportedly extensive behind-the-scenes negotiations, the companies refused to cut prices. The resulting wage settlement exceeded the guideposts, and automobile prices were not decreased, hence both the workers and the companies reaped the benefits of the industry's above-average productivity. Sheahan's analysis of this "episode" led him to conclude that it "fairly well consecrated defeat for the idea of getting price reductions in industries for which productivity gains are above average." [23]

On other occasions between 1962 and 1966, the guideposts were invoked publicly by the council in industries covering several broad and largely key sectors of the economy, including construction, aluminum, copper, hides, petroleum, cigarettes, molybdenum—and government employee salaries.

THE LIMITS OF GUIDEPOST POLICY

Space precludes a full discussion of the various successes, partial successes, and failures of the guideposts. Certainly there is no consensus among economists as to the extent to which the guideposts have worked. Most analysts agree, however, that the guideposts are entitled to some credit for the record price stability that played so important a role in the sustained economic growth following 1961. While it is especially difficult to pinpoint their effectiveness since about mid-1965, when excess *demand* began placing added pressures on prices, the guideposts themselves were not to be blamed for that difficulty. They cannot be criticized for failing to stop inflation caused by excess demand, since, of course, they were never designed to cope with that problem.

This much seems clear, however. In view of the very real

[23] Sheahan, *op. cit.*, p. 41.

problem presented, one that necessitated some form of restraint on parties with great discretionary pricing power, the experiment with wage-price guideposts between 1961 and 1965 may be considered a qualified success. Even during the period of demand-pull inflation of 1968, the office of the president was used successfully to talk down price increases in steel and automobiles. If the price increases originally announced by these industries in the summer of 1968 had gone into effect, they would have added fuel to the price spiral. However, when the government announced in early 1969 that it had abandoned the "guidepost" philosophy, it encouraged key decisionmakers to increase prices—a fact immediately reflected in a rapid rise in wholesale industrial prices. Simply put, this new policy—actually a reversion to pre-1962 policy—shifted the nation's Phillips curve to the right. As a result, we will have to accept a higher level of unemployment before price stability is restored.

In evaluating the possible efficacy of a guideposts policy, however, it should be recognized that there are very severe limits to its effectiveness. First, it is an essentially voluntary program, one based on education, exhortation, or admonition by the council and, in special cases, by the president. By its very nature, there is a serious limit on the frequency with which such a policy can be applied. In nearly every public confrontation, the prestige of the council and, to varying degrees, that of the president, are placed on the line. A series of failures, or even one or two major failures, would immediately weaken the government's position in future negotiations. Hence the guideposts must necessarily be used rather sparingly.

Second, the potential usefulness of the guideposts is limited to certain kinds of industries, the ideal case for their application being the very large industry that sells a homogenous product. It is this factor which at least partly explains why the programs worked most effectively in steel, aluminum, and copper. When an industry sells numerous essentially differentiated products, for example, breakfast cereals, it is next to impossible to invoke the guideposts. The cereals industry is one of the country's most profitable industries, and the leading companies in it have much pricing discretion. But one can hardly imagine a president requesting General Mills to roll back the price of Cheerios or Wheaties.

Consider the drug industry. Here the leading manufacturers enjoy wide price discretion and are more profitable than the members of any other major American industry. Yet literally thousands of ethical and proprietary drugs are sold under a myriad of brands. Similar problems of application exist across a broad spectrum of consumer industries where product differentiation is commonplace and where firms frequently enjoy great discretion over price. Perhaps for this reason alone as many as one-fourth of all manufacturing industries are essentially unreachable under the guideposts.

Third, the government has more "tools of persuasion" available to it in some industries than it has in others. In copper and aluminum, the government was able to back up its plea for price restraint by releasing supplies on the market from government stockpiles of these products. But these two are about the only industries where this policy could be followed. In some other cases—in steel, for example—admonition could be backed up by government procurement policy. On the other hand, in petroleum, import quotas could be adjusted if the domestic prices became too high. In any case the number of opportunities to use procurement or international trade policies is quite limited. Moreover, frequent resort to such strategies might incite severe public criticism.

Fourth, an industry might be able to avoid the invocation of the guidelines by changing the *pattern* of its price increases. Instead of raising all prices across the board, it might raise the price on only a few items at a time. Because no single increase has much of an impact, the industry would then stand a better chance of "getting by" with its increases. In the aggregate, however, a series of such "selective" price increases could have the same impact as a single, large, across-the-board increase.

Fifth, labor unions are, in general, more susceptible to the application of the guideposts than are business concerns. Wage negotiations occur rather infrequently and are quite readily translated into specific dollar amounts, factors that make it easy to determine whether an increase exceeds the guideposts. In the case of the business enterprises, on the other hand, there is the added question of whether productivity in the particular industry has been above or below the national average. One result of this complication, as noted in the case of automobiles, is that the guideposts have been almost totally ineffective in inducing price *decreases* in industries with above-average productivity gains.

Sixth, it is difficult to apply the guideposts in industries composed of numerous submarkets subjected to different supply-and-demand conditions. As noted in Chapter 6, for a period of ten years bread bakers in the state of Washington fixed prices at 15 percent to 20 percent above the national average. The guideposts can do little about such isolated markets. Similarly, although bread prices rose in most American cities during 1966, they did so by varying amounts; after the increases prices varied considerably from city to city.[24] In such circumstances, it is not possible to roll back prices across the board by using the techniques applied in steel. Even if some of the price increases were unwarranted, rolling them all back would necessarily result in great inequities.

It would be possible, of course, to add other factors that seriously limit the scope of the wage-price guideposts as an effective instrument in restraining seller-induced inflation. A few of them have been made explicit here so as not to delude some into believing that this policy alone is an adequate instrument for restraining the use of significant market power.

It should be noted that the Council of Economic Advisers itself has never been so deluded. From the outset, it has repeatedly emphasized that the guideposts have only a limited application, explaining since their inception that primary reliance

---

[24] See Federal Trade Commission, *Economic Report on Milk and Bread Prices* (Washington, D.C.: Federal Trade Commission, November 1966).

must be placed on effectively competitive markets, not on government controls, whether semivoluntary or compulsory.

In this connection, it might be well to recall the context in which the council presented the guideposts in its 1962 report. They were included as one part of a discussion entitled "Policies Affecting Price Behavior," a section that began by stating explicitly that price stability must be maintained within an "environment of dynamic competition." This section of the report also emphasized other related policy goals: "Public policies to encourage economy-wide competition not only contribute to the goal of price stability; they also promote efficiency and the advance of productivity." [25] Further, the 1962 report concluded a section headed "Policies to Foster Market Competition" with an explanation of why antitrust policy toward price fixing, anticompetitive mergers, and industrial concentration is an essential part of a long-run policy aimed at achieving price stability and economic growth.[26] It was only after these discussions that the council set forth the guideposts as a technique for dealing with the "special" circumstances where industries had discretionary market power.

Subsequent reports of the council have reemphasized that primary reliance must be placed on market competition to maintain proper price-cost relation and allocative efficiency. The 1969 report, for example, emphasized that "A continuing program of antitrust actions can increase competition and contribute to improved overall price performance at high employment." [27]

President Johnson's Cabinet Committee on Price Stability, in its final report to the president, emphasized that competition policy was an essential part of anti-inflation policy. It concluded:

[25] *Annual Report of the Council of Economic Advisers* (Washington, D.C.: Council of Economic Advisers, January 1962), p. 183.

[26] *Ibid.*, pp. 184–185.

[27] *Annual Report of the Council of Economic Advisers* (Washington, D.C.: Council of Economic Advisers, January 1969), p. 107.

We recommend vigorous enforcement of the antitrust laws as essential for reducing further the inflationary effects of discretionary power. Only to the extent that we maintain effective market competition can we continue to place primary reliance on private decision-makers in our quests for high employment, rapid economic growth, and price stability.

The competitive vitality of the American economy may give it a comparative advantage over other nations in the battle against inflation. The postwar experiences of a number of other countries may be instructive in this regard. Some western European nations have adopted more formal kinds of controls —commonly called "prices and incomes policies"—than the United States guideposts policy. Yet, despite inflationary pressures in the United States over the past decade, consumer prices have risen more rapidly in other leading nations than in the United States, thus indicating that more basic forces than the kinds of controls a country selects determine the level of price inflation. Very possibly, however, one of the "other" im-

CONSUMER PRICE INCREASES BETWEEN
1960 AND 1968

Japan	54%
Italy	36
Netherlands	33
France	32
United Kingdom	32
Germany	22
Canada	21
United States	17

portant forces affecting prices is the relatively greater effectiveness of price competition in the United States than in most other nations.

Quite clearly, then, the attainment of the objectives of the Employment Act of 1946 depends heavily on the maintenance of effective market competition. By the same token, however, when market competition does break down, alternative methods of social control will inevitably be imposed. The guideposts thus represent an intermediate step between complete reliance on the market, on the one hand, and direct government regulation of prices and wages, on the other. Because the guideposts can be invoked in only a limited number of situations and because American experience demonstrates that direct controls are, except in times of national crises, an extremely unpalatable alternative, primary reliance must necessarily be placed on the market.

The United States will doubtless continue to experiment with guideposts and alternative forms of social control. As in other areas of economic and social policy, the country will likely follow an essentially pragmatic approach, one based on what experience proves to be both workable and equitable. The nature and extent of voluntary or formal price controls will ultimately depend, of course, on the degree of effectiveness of market competition in disciplining private economic power. To the extent that the self-regulating forces of market competition are diminished, greater formal government controls will inevitably follow. It is just that simple.

In closing, the interaction of economic growth and competitive markets should again be stressed. The enormous size and rapid growth of the economy have opened new opportunities for effective competition. Hence, not only have competitive markets played a key role in the success of the "new economics," but the latter has, in turn, done much to promote the opportunities for more effective competition.

CHAPTER 8

Public Policy Toward Monopoly: Theory of Business Regulation

HISTORICAL ORIGINS

Every society must adopt a system of social control over its economy. One alternative is government ownership and operation of economic enterprise. At the other extreme, economic enterprise may be privately owned and operated entirely independent of government control. The latter policy of so-called laissez faire, either implicitly or explicitly, places complete reliance on market forces to achieve private performance in the public interest. Between these polar extremes lies a spectrum of public regulation of private enterprise.

Americans have long had a healthy suspicion of uncontrolled economic power, whether held by private or by public interests. The Jeffersonian-Jacksonian economic philosophy reflected and articulated this suspicion; it did not create it. Even before the founding of the republic, the American Colonies were sensitive to questions of economic power. In 1641 a Massachusetts legislature decreed that "there shall be no monopolies granted or allowed among us but of such new inventions as are profitable to the country, and that for a short time."

During nearly 200 years of experience, the United States has had a "mixed" economic system. It is a common mistake of those not familiar with American history to assume that government intervention is of recent origin. But as the prominent economic historian Forrest Hill has observed, "If we were able to disregard or discount for changes in the scale and complexity of the economy and the government, we might find that over the past 140 or 170 years the role of government has not increased very greatly in relative size or significance."

But it was not until after the Industrial Revolution began restructuring the previously simple economic order that a formal body of federal law was created to cope with the new and powerful economic interests. The people were puzzled and disturbed by events they did not understand and over which they had little control. John M. Harlan, associate justice of the Supreme Court, writing in 1911, characterized the mood of the country in the late nineteenth century:

> All who recall the condition of the country in 1890 will remember that there was everywhere, among the people generally, a deep feeling of unrest. The nation had been rid of human slavery—fortunately, as all now feel—but the conviction was universal that the country was in real danger from another kind of slavery sought to be fastened on the American people; namely, the slavery that would result from aggregations of capital in the hands of a few individuals and corporations controlling, for their own profit and advantage exclusively, the entire business of the country, including the production and sale of the necessities of life.[1]

Because the existing methods of social control were inadequate to deal with the new economic order, Americans devised two new forms of control. First, where economic realities seemed to rule out the possibility of competitively organized markets, the Congress, acting under the commerce clause of the Constitution, created public regulatory bodies to oversee the behavior of these so-called natural monopoly industries.

[1] *Standard Oil Co. of New Jersey* v. *United States*, 221 U.S. 83 (1911).

(Many states also created such regulatory bodies.) The first such federal agency was the Interstate Commerce Commission, established in 1887.

The second approach involved the enactment of a number of statutes designed to preserve and enhance competition in those industries where economic conditions did not make monopoly inevitable. These statutes are called the antitrust laws, named after the "trusts," which were a common form of monopoly at the time the first act was passed in 1890.

Americans have taken an essentially pragmatic approach in exercising social control over economic activity. Where experience has demonstrated that competition is not feasible, economic activity has been conducted either by the government itself—local, state or federal—or by private enterprise regulated by government authorities. Examples of government-performed functions are the postal service, education, and, in some cases, electrical and other utilities—for example, TVA and locally owned water works. The primary areas of privately owned and operated enterprise regulated by local, state, or federal authorities are electrical utilities, communications, railroads, air transportation, insurance, and banking.

As shown in Table 8.1, in 1966 only 1.3 percent of national income originated from government enterprise and 14.1 percent from industries regulated to some degree by governmental authorities. Most regulated industries are so-called natural monopoly industries—transportation (4 percent), communications (2 percent), electric and other utilities (2 percent), banking (1.6 percent), and insurance (0.9 percent). A limited number of competitively structured industries are regulated to achieve special public policy objectives—some natural resource industries (2.2 percent) and some segments of the agriculture industries (1.4 percent).

The economic performance of the industries mentioned above is regulated by either local, state, or federal agencies or commissions. In almost all other segments of the economy, market forces are the primary regulator of economic activity. This latter area, which accounts for the great majority of na-

TABLE 8.1 / PERCENTAGE OF NATIONAL INCOME ORIGINATING IN GOVERNMENT ENTERPRISE AND REGULATED INDUSTRIES, 1966

Government enterprise	Percentage of National Income
Federal	0.9
State	0.4
Regulated industries	
Transportation	
Railroads	1.1
Local and highway passenger	0.3
Highway freight	1.4
Water transportation	0.4
Air transportation	0.9
Communication	2.0
Electric, gas, and other utilities	2.0
Commercial banking	1.6
Insurance	0.9
Crude oil and natural gas	2.2
Agriculture*	1.4
Total government enterprise and regulated	15.5

* Includes only the regulated portion.
SOURCE: U.S. Department of Commerce, *Statistical Abstract of the United States.*

tional income, is the major area of concern of public policy toward competition.

This classification is, of course, a greatly oversimplified separation between the "controlled" or "regulated" sectors of the economy and the "market" sectors. First, even in the regulated sector, great reliance is placed on market forces. Many aspects of banking behavior, for example, are not controlled or specified by the regulatory authorities. Government regulation consists mainly of protecting lenders and investors by guaranteeing deposits, controlling the quality of assets, placing maximum rates on interest paid lenders, and limiting new entry.

On the other hand, interest rates charged borrowers are not controlled by regulatory authorities, except for usury laws of states that place a ceiling on interest rates. Many aspects of performance in the so-called regulated industries are not regulated. Rather, heavy reliance is placed on market forces to insure satisfactory performance. This explains why antitrust policy includes certain responsibilities in the regulated segments of the economy as well as in the unregulated.

Second, Americans have not relied solely upon market forces to insure adequate performance in the unregulated segments of the economy. Public authority has been exerted to set minimum wages, unemployment compensation, medical benefits for the aged, retirement benefits, and other regulations. Additionally, government monetary and fiscal policy has been employed to achieve full employment and to stimulate economic growth. These various policies involve substantial and far-reaching government intervention in the workings of the economy. Importantly, however, although these policies have an impact on business enterprises as well as individuals, they generally do not involve direct specification of basic price and output decisions of business enterprises.

Put differently, while these broader government policies affect the environment of business enterprises, business decisions are made predominantly by private enterprises responding to market forces. As a result, the organization and planning of industrial production is done by hundreds of thousands of individual business units without any central direction by government authority. This is what is meant when it is stated that market forces are the primary "regulator" of the performance of the business unit.

In view of the central role played by market forces in organizing the American economic system, it is not surprising that public policy has long been concerned with the operation of the competitive process. Beginning in 1890 the United States enacted a series of statutes intended to maintain competition as an effective regulator of economic activity. The laws designed to accomplish this objective are called the antitrust laws. The following chapter will discuss these laws and their enforcement. But first a few words about the philosophy underlying the antitrust approach to industrial regulation.

THEORY OF ANTITRUST

The basic purpose of the antitrust laws is to maintain sufficiently competitive market structure and market conduct to insure that private enterprise performs in a socially acceptable manner. At the heart of this approach is the assumption that by controlling or modifying certain aspects of industrial structure and competitive conduct, the public can avoid government intervention in the economically and politically hazardous thicket of specifying industrial performance. Hence the antitrust approach is different from other forms of business "regulation." It does not tell businessmen what and how much to produce or at what price to sell their products. Rather, the antitrust approach is directed at maintaining sufficient competition in the market place so that market forces will "compel" desirable economic performance.

Much antitrust enforcement involves formulating rules that govern the ways in which the competitive game is played. In Chapter 2 it was shown that economic theory suggests, and empirical studies verify, that *market structure* plays a powerful role in determining or conditioning *business conduct,* and that *business conduct,* in turn, determines the ultimate quality of *industrial performance*. This, of course, is not to say that an industry's structure and conduct are the only factors determining ultimate performance. But available empirical evidence indicates that structural characteristics such as the height of entry barriers facing potential competitors, the degree of product differentiation, and the level of market concentration are *always* of some importance, and often of decisive importance, in determining industry performance.

It should not be inferred, however, that analysis of industry structure involves no more than counting the noses of competitors. Increasingly, sophisticated exploration of the technological and other forces underlying industrial organization is essential to a realistic interpretation of structural developments.

Similarly, there is general agreement that certain forms of business conduct result in undesirable performance. For example, restrictive or collusive agreements among competitors may result in monopoly pricing even in industries that would otherwise generate competitive prices. Other forms of conduct may adversely affect market structure and, thereby, ultimate industry performance. Predatory pricing is an example. Although in the short run such conduct may give consumers low prices, in the long run it may also destroy competitors and result in higher prices.

Various antitrust laws are directed at the first two of the market structure-conduct-performance trilogy. Section 1 of the Sherman Act prohibits certain forms of anticompetitive conduct, particularly restraints of trade, such as conspiracies to fix prices. Similarly, Section 2 of the Clayton Act (the Robinson-Patman Act) prohibits anticompetitive price discrimination, and Section 5 of the Federal Trade Commission Act deals with unfair competition. On the other hand, Section 2 of the Sherman Act may be used to bring about structural changes by breaking up monopolies. Section 7 of the Clayton Act may prevent the emergence of anticompetitive market structures by preventing certain kinds of mergers. (These acts and their enforcement are discussed in detail in the following chapter.)

The important point is that antitrust policy does not involve exhaustive investigation or analysis of *all* the factors that may conceivably have a bearing on industrial performance, nor does it involve direct specification of desired performance. This is both the strength and the weakness of the antitrust approach. Its strength derives from the fact that a maximum effect may flow from a minimum of government intervention. It is not necessary to assemble and maintain a vast bureaucracy that exercises continued intervention in and surveillance of business affairs. But this is precisely what is required when public policy has as its objective the identification and implementation of what constitutes desirable performance. To do this job well requires an enormous volume of regulatory resources. For example, the Interstate Commerce Commission, whose major responsibilities consist of setting of rates and other performance characteristics, has twice as many employees as the combined employees in antitrust enforcement at the Federal Trade Commission and the Department of Justice. And, importantly, the ICC has responsibility for just part of the field of transportation. (As shown in Table 8.1, industries regulated by the ICC account for less than 4 percent of national income.) Quite clearly, in relation to the antitrust approach, direct specification of industry performance requires a vast amount of government resources and intervention into the day-to-day affairs of business.

But while the great virtue of the antitrust approach is that it requires a minimum of regulatory resources and intervention into business affairs, this fact also makes it an easy mark for its critics. Because there are not always precise causal links among market structure, conduct, and performance, rules of law controlling or modifying market structure and conduct are necessarily vulnerable to adverse criticism. Empirical evidence concerning the precise interrelationships among structure, conduct, and performance leaves much to be desired. Consequently, nearly every rule of law dealing with important problems is open to critical comment, because it conflicts with some economist's or businessman's conception of the true economic wisdom on the matter.

Nor is this criticism a novelty of the 1960s. In every decade since 1890 some economists and others have urged abandonment or substantial modification of the antitrust laws on grounds of obsolescence. They have argued that, while antitrust may have had its place in 1890, the inexorable advance of technology has rendered archaic traditional competitive concepts.[2] There may well be some substance to this belief. But

2 Chapter 10 discusses in some detail the most recent attack on the antitrust approach to regulation.

merely asserting it does not make it so. As noted in Chapter 4, recent empirical studies give little support for the arguments that invention, innovation, and economic progress demand vast industrial complexes with considerable market power. These findings strongly suggest that the empirical basis for the antitrust approach to business "regulation" is at least as strong today as it has ever been.

Much of the antitrust approach involves placing restraints on certain competitive practices tending to frustrate the "market test" of business success. The merger law is an example. When a company secures a strong market position by internal growth, the presumption is that—unless it has used predatory or similar tactics—it has bested its rivals in a fair fight and is therefore entitled to reap the rewards of victory. But when the company does so by merger, no similar presumption is warranted. Therefore, a merger that substantially lessens competition is illegal.

In an assessment of the adequacy of the antitrust approach, this policy must be weighed against its alternatives. Obviously, complete abandonment of business "regulation" is not a realistic or a desirable alternative. Economic history states eloquently that there are no "natural" economic laws which make the competitive process self-perpetuating. The only alternative to the antitrust approach—in modern America—is more *direct* regulation of business affairs, involving direct specification of industrial performance in various important respects, or direct government ownership. Although these alternatives have been pursued in industries of natural monopolies, the United States experience demonstrates the great economic and political difficulties confronting the attempt to do a satisfactory job of direct regulation or government operation even in industries with quite simple technological and market problems.

Moreover, American experience over the past seventy-eight years—since passage of the Sherman Act in 1890—demonstrates that the antitrust route of regulation works tolerably well. Admittedly some intractable positions of market power cannot be dissipated by antitrust policy alone, and other important industries are so poorly structured that they leave much to be desired in terms of industrial performance. But, importantly, such industries are the exceptions rather than the rule. Most American industries—outside those under direct regulation—are effectively competitive. Nor has there been any persistent tendency toward increased market concentration in the postwar years, largely because of intensive anti-merger enforcement.

Even some seemingly sophisticated observers of day-to-day antitrust enforcement often view it as a direct assault on big business or, worse still, on the free enterprise system itself.

But antitrust is basically probusiness, because it is antimonopoly. To believe that it is antibusiness is to believe that monopoly is probusiness. Much criticism of antitrust results from misunderstanding of this approach. It involves primarily adversary procedures and is essentially negative—it tells businessmen what they cannot do. Nor do the antitrust agencies give businesses things of value, such as licenses and rate increases. On the contrary, every antitrust lawsuit alleges that the business or the individuals involved have committed a wrong against society in that they have violated an antitrust statute. In a word, they are charged with law violations. Understandably, those so charged do not appreciate the publicity associated with such charges, nor do they relish the idea that a force external to the market—the antitrust authority—threatens to place constraints on their conduct. Additional hostility may result as the issues contained in a complaint are tested by a judicial process wherein a government authority and business are pitted as adversaries. Again, the untutored observer may view such adversary proceedings as proof positive that antitrust represents a fundamental attack on established business institutions or as a basic conflict between government and business.

Such an interpretation is precisely false. It mistakes independence and arm's-length dealing between antitrust authorities and business as evidence of open hostility and disagreement on the basic goals of our society. Again, those critical of antitrust must evaluate it in terms of the alternatives. Would they really prefer business and government to become partners in the rule-making and rule-enforcing processes? Perhaps those desiring a "government-business partnership" in the antitrust area are using the term as a euphemism for either government control of business or business control of government. Of course, most who urge such a partnership have no well-thought-out notion of what they mean by it; others employ it as a public relations gimmick in the hope that fervent and repeated cries for such a partnership will themselves create an environment conducive to amity in government-business relations. But to resort to a sports analogy, who would propose that the players join with the umpires in a "player-umpire partnership"?

This is not to say that much cannot be done to minimize needless misunderstanding, hostility, and uncertainty under the antitrust laws. For example, in the past few years the antitrust authorities have adopted a series of programs designed to provide greater guidance to business in some of the gray areas of antitrust and have instituted industry-wide enforcement programs aimed at eliminating, where possible, the discriminatory features of the case-by-case approach.

All business uncertainty, however, cannot be eliminated in antitrust any more than in other areas of business decision—certainty, too, has its price. The businessman may well recall the aphorism, "better no rules than cruel rules." Ultimately, individual businesses or groups of businesses will disagree with an antitrust agency's interpretation of the law. Then the adversary approach must be resorted to in charting new rules of law and in enforcing established ones. Adversary proceedings involve impersonal, arm's-length dealings resulting in rules of law rather than rules of men. Such independence and impersonality permit antitrust to work in the public interest, because, in the long run, this approach requires a minimum of government intervention into the decision-making process. The counterpart to the "independence" of the antitrust agencies is the "independence" of the business enterprise. It means that as the rules of competition are spelled out, the vast majority of a company's market decisions are independent of government intervention. As a result, market forces serve as the primary regulator of business decisions.

In conclusion, it should be emphasized that American antitrust policy is not rooted solely in economic objectives. This uniquely American institution is also rooted in the Jeffersonian philosophy that vast concentrations of economic power weaken the fabric of democratic institutions. President John F. Kennedy articulated this philosophy when he said, "the free market is not only a more efficient decision maker than the wisest central planning body, but even more important, the free market keeps economic power widely dispersed [and] this is a vital underpinning of our democratic system."

While the various antitrust laws were at least partly adopted in the expectation or hope of attaining political and social objectives as well as economic ones, the laws themselves are concerned primarily with competitive processes and are therefore interpreted within an economic framework.

CHAPTER 9

Public Policy Toward Monopoly: Application of Antitrust Laws

ANTITRUST LAWS

The Sherman Act of 1890 was passed in the heyday of the "trusts," and its provisions were aimed at the monopolistic practices common to that day. Significantly, whereas in 1887 the Interstate Commerce Commission was created to *regulate* a "natural" monopoly, the Sherman Act was aimed at *preventing* the formation of monopoly.

The decision to rely on competition, wherever possible, as the chief regulating force in the economy marked a significant step in United States economic-political history. In the nearly eight decades following 1890, primary reliance has been placed on competitive market forces instead of on direct government regulation in the greater part of the American economy. As the Supreme Court observed in 1963:

> Subject to narrow qualification, it is surely the case that competition is our fundamental national policy, offering as it does the only alternative to the cartelization or governmental regimentation of large portions of the economy.[1]

[1] *United States* v. *Philadelphia National Bank,* 374 U.S. 321, 372 (1963).

The Sherman Act is a brief yet comprehensive statute. Although the act makes no reference to competition, it is vitally concerned with protecting the competitive process.

Section 1 of the act is aimed at practices that eliminate competition among existing rivals. It does so by rendering illegal "every contract, combination in the form of trust or otherwise, or conspiracy, in restraint of trade. . . ." Section 2 of the act makes it illegal to "monopolize, or attempt to monopolize . . . any part of the trade or commerce among the several states or with foreign nations. . . ." This language has been interpreted to prohibit a variety of practices, such as price fixing agreements, mergers, and predatory pricing, that transform an otherwise competitively structured market into one giving market power to business.

The Sherman Act is both a criminal and a civil statute. The criminal provisions of the act penalize illegal conduct through the imposition of fines and imprisonment. In civil suits, the government may ask the courts to order divestiture, compulsory licensing of patents, or other actions required to provide appropriate relief. The Antitrust Division of the Department of Justice has the responsibility of enforcing the act. A private party may also bring suit under the Sherman Act, and may sue to recover treble damages for the injury it has suffered from practices found to be in violation of the act.

Early experience with enforcement of the Sherman Act demonstrated that competition could be injured by practices that fell short of creating full-blown monopoly. To remedy this defect of the Sherman Act, the Congress enacted the Clayton Act in 1914. In a word, the latter act was aimed at incipient monopoly rather than full-blown monopoly.

The Clayton Act was directed at four specific anticompetitive practices: price discrimination, tying contracts and exclusive dealing, mergers, and interlocking directorates.

The Federal Trade Commission Act of 1914 created the Federal Trade Commission as an independent, quasi-judicial agency. The commission is composed of five commissioners appointed by the president, with the advice and consent of the senate. Each commissioner is appointed for seven years, and no more than three commissioners may belong to the same political party. The president designates as chairman one of the five commissioners.

Congress contemplated that the FTC would develop special expertise about the organization and the behavior of American business. FTC was designed to complement the enforcement effort of the Department of Justice, with which it shared enforcement of the newly created Clayton Act.

Section 5 of the act empowered the commission to prohibit "unfair methods of competition." This broad language was designed to prohibit anticompetitive practices not specifically prohibited by the Sherman and the Clayton Acts. The founders of the act anticipated that the words "unfair competition" would "grow and broaden and mold themselves to meet circumstances as they arise."

The Federal Trade Commission has the authority, subject to judicial review, to issue cease-and-desist orders prohibiting companies from continuing practices declared to be unfair methods of competition. Private parties cannot enforce the FTC Act.

In addition to enforcing the antitrust statutes, the FTC also has broad authority, under Section 6 of the FTC Act, to undertake economic inquiries into the conduct and structure of American business. This authority has been used to undertake inquiries providing the basis for remedial trade regulation legislation, for example, the Packers and Stockyards Act of 1921, the Securities Act of 1933, the Securities Exchange Act of 1934, the Public Utility Holding Company Act of 1935, the Robinson-Patman Act of 1936, and the Celler-Kefauver Act of 1950. Most recently the commission has undertaken a broad-scale inquiry into the problem posed by conglomerate mergers.

ENFORCEMENT OF ANTITRUST STATUTES

Price Fixing

Price fixing and related efforts by private parties are illegal per se under the antitrust laws. It is no defense to argue that the price fixed is a "reasonable" one. The Supreme Court disposed of the "reasonableness" argument several decades ago when it stated:

> The power to fix prices, whether reasonably exercised or not, involves power to control the market and to fix arbitrary and unreasonable prices. The reasonable price fixed today may, due to economic and business changes become the unreasonable price of tomorrow.[2]

Although it is impossible to ferret out all price-fixing agreements, the threat of antitrust prosecution has been a powerful deterrent to price-fixing arrangements. Because the penalty provisions of the act include imprisonment, fines, and treble damages, conspiracy can be a risky and costly business. For example, in the recent electrical conspiracy case,[3] several officers found guilty of fixing prices were given jail terms, and the various defendants paid fines of $1,926,000. Moreover, to date, the defendants reportedly have paid treble damages in excess of $500 million. The federal government received $8,918,650 in damages for the inflated prices it paid for electrical equipment (particularly purchases by the TVA) as a result of this price-fixing conspiracy. Recent convictions in a drug conspiracy case are likely to result in damage payments exceeding $100 million (see Chapter 6).

In antitrust actions striking down price-fixing arrangements, the consumer receives considerable returns from his invest-

2 *U.S. v. Trenton Potteries Co.,* 273 U.S. 392 (1927).
3 See Chapter 6.

ment. For example, the damage payments received by parties injured by the electrical conspiracy alone were twice as large as the combined antimonopoly expenditures of the Federal Trade Commission and the Department of Justice since 1890. And consumers would very likely pay billions of dollars more for the necessities of life were it not for strict enforcement of the antitrust laws against price fixing.

The law against business conspiracy extends not only to price-fixing agreements but to other forms of business restraints. For example, on January 10, 1969, the government challenged General Motors and other automobile companies for allegedly conspiring to restrain trade and commerce in motor vehicle air pollution control equipment. The automobile companies allegedly agreed, among other things, "on at least three separate occasions to attempt to delay the installation of motor vehicle air pollution control equipment." This matter is currently before the court.

Law of Monopoly

Many important antimonopoly cases have been brought under the Sherman Act. Several early cases resulted in breaking up key monopolies. Perhaps the most important suit involved the Standard Oil Company of New Jersey. In 1911 the Supreme Court ordered the dissolution of Standard Oil, which through acquisitions and predatory acts had acquired control of more than seventy petroleum companies. In the same year the court ordered the dissolution of the American Tobacco Company. These two decisions not only restructured the oil and the tobacco industries but also set forth the "rule of reason," which distinguished between good trusts and bad trusts. The Supreme Court concluded that the oil and the tobacco trusts were bad trusts, because they had been achieved through predatory and other monopolizing practices.

Applying the "rule of reason" to the United States Steel combination, the court concluded in 1920 that United States

Steel was a good trust. The court found no fault in this combination because, "It resorted to none of the brutalities or tyrannies that the cases illustrate of other combinations." [4]

The most important monopoly decision in recent decades involved the Aluminum Company of America (Alcoa), which had held a virtual monopoly of virgin aluminum for over fifty years. Alcoa's monopoly originated in basic patents and was sustained by various monopolizing techniques. In finding the monopoly illegal in 1945 Judge Learned Hand concluded that Alcoa's 90 percent share of virgin ingot production constituted a monopoly under the Sherman Act. The court subsequently severed Alcoa's ties with Aluminium Limited, of Canada, and required Alcoa to open the industry to new competition by licensing other domestic producers under its patents. Because of subsequent disposal of the government wartime aluminum plants to competitors and the entry of entirely new firms, the number of aluminum companies has increased from two to seven over the past two decades. Thus America's leading monopoly outside the regulated industries was dissipated by court actions and complementary government policies fostering competition. (The Reynolds Metals Company entered aluminum production during World War II with the aid of the government. After the war the government disposed of several of its wartime aluminum plants to Reynolds and to Kaiser Aluminum and Chemical Corporation. During the 1950s government stockpile procurement policy was applied to encourage three additional companies to enter the industry. During the 1960s two additional companies entered without government assistance.)

Another recent important monopoly case involved United Shoe Machinery Company, which had held a virtual monopoly in its field for many decades. In 1947 the government challenged this monopoly position, and in 1953 a District Court held that United Shoe had violated Section 2 of the Sherman Act by monopolizing the manufacture of shoe machinery. The court found that "(1) defendant has, and exercises, such over-

[4] *U.S.* v. *United States Steel Corp.*, 251 U.S. 417 (1920).

whelming strength in the shoe machinery market that it controls that market, (2) this strength excludes some potential, and limits some actual, competition, and (3) this strength is not attributable solely to defendant's ability, economies of scale, research, natural advantages, and adaptation to inevitable economic laws."

Although the government had asked the court to break up the monopoly, the court refused to do so. Rather, it imposed on United Shoe a variety of restrictions and conditions designed "to recreate a competitive market." The court provided further, however, that if competition were not revived by January, 1965, the government could petition the court for further relief. Although United Shoe's market position had declined in the intervening years, it still held a dominant position by 1965, when the government petitioned the court for further relief. Following a Supreme Court decision in 1968 favoring the government, United Shoe agreed to a consent judgment in early 1969 to divest assets, reducing its share of the domestic shoe machinery market to no more than 33 percent.

The Sherman Act has served to prevent the emergence of monopolies in unregulated United States industries. Inspection of all large American industries reveals that none is occupied by a single enterprise. But while the Sherman Act has prevented the emergence of classical, single-company monopoly, it has not, to date, proved an effective instrument to cope with hard-core oligopolistic industries. Its main impact in such industries has been to help keep the door open to potential new entrants and to provide a shield against predatory behavior designed to destroy less powerful competitors threatening to erode the market position of dominant enterprises.

On January 17, 1969, the Department of Justice initiated what well could be the most significant monopoly case ever brought under the Sherman Act. The government complaint charges International Business Machines Corporation (the world's largest manufacturer of information-handling machines) with monopolizing and attempting to monopolize the general digital computer market. Significantly, several of IBM's competitors have also brought private antitrust suits against IBM. The ultimate outcome of this litigation could have a profound impact on the future of competition in this vital industry.

Law of Mergers

Whereas the Sherman Act is directed at monopoly and monopolizing conduct, the Clayton Act is aimed at incipient monopoly—or, as its authors put it, "to catch the weed in the seed." Limitation of space permits discussion of the enforcement of only one of the various provisions of the law, that dealing with mergers.

Section 7 of the Clayton Act, as amended by the Celler-Kefauver Act of 1950, is directed at mergers that threaten competition. Following passage of the Sherman Act of 1890, a great merger movement engulfed much of United States industry. When a company made so many mergers as to create a monopoly, this action violated the Sherman Act. Individual mergers that involved only a partial step toward monopoly generally fell outside the Sherman Act. Section 7 was designed to cope with such mergers. The original Clayton Act covered only mergers in which one company acquired the stock of another company, but left untouched mergers accomplished by the purchase of another company's assets. This so-called asset loophole was closed by the Celler-Kefauver Act of 1950.

It cannot be emphasized too strongly that the Celler-Kefauver Act applies legal standards different from those of the Sherman Act. The former act is aimed at those mergers which *may* substantially lessen competition or *tend* to create a monopoly. The words "may" and "tend" are crucial, because they make operative the fact that the new law was designed to strike at monopoly in its incipiency, not just at clear-cut monopoly-creating mergers. This point is a fundamental distinction between the Celler-Kefauver Act and the Sherman Act. The Celler-Kefauver Act purposely was designed to come into play *before* competition has actually and demonstrably been injured to the extent that a merger has conferred substantial market power on an acquiring company.

What is the economic rationale underlying this seemingly harsh public policy toward growth by merger? Economic history teaches that mergers have played a central role in restructuring many United States industries. Conversely, few industries have become highly concentrated through internal growth alone. When a company grows by internal growth—by building new capacity and by increasing consumer acceptance for its products—there is always a "market test" of their success.[6] This is not necessarily true when growth involves mergers. When a company grows by combining with others, there is no clear-cut market test to determine if the resulting industry structure is based on economic efficiency. Because of this, the antitrust laws treat growth by merger differently from internal growth.

Since 1950 the Federal Trade Commission and the Department of Justice have issued over 200 merger complaints challenging over 800 mergers.[7] Most of these cases involved acquisitions by the 500 largest manufacturing concerns.[8] By 1966, fully 62 percent of the manufacturing corporations with assets exceeding $1 billion had been challenged in one or more of their acquisitions, and 29 percent of those with assets between $250 million and $1 billion had been so challenged. Practically no mergers by small companies have been challenged.

[6] That is to say, if it has used "fair" methods of competition, it can be assumed that even a dominant company has achieved its position because of superior efficiency. This is not to say, of course, that monopolies rooted solely in economies of scale do not pose an economic problem. As noted earlier, a number of "natural monopoly" industries are regulated by the government.

[7] See Willard F. Mueller, *The Celler-Kefauver Act: Sixteen Years of Enforcement* (Washington, D.C.: U.S. House of Representatives, Staff Report of the Antitrust Subcommittee, Committee on the Judiciary, October 16, 1967).

[8] *Ibid.*

Consequences of Merger Policy

Enforcement policy may have either a direct or an indirect effect on industrial organization. Challenging and undoing particular mergers has an immediate and a direct impact. Although there are a number of notable examples in which important mergers have been blocked or undone, the chief impact of enforcement policy is the deterrent effect of threatened prosecution. This aspect of the policy is most evident in horizontal mergers, that is, mergers between direct competitors. Public policy has virtually stopped such mergers by large companies. As noted earlier, whereas in 1948–1951 about 41 percent of all mergers were horizontal, by 1968 only 4 percent were of this type (see Chapter 5).

The prevention of substantial horizontal mergers is especially critical because a substantial merger or a series of small ones can rapidly increase the level of industry concentration. When industry sales become highly concentrated among a few sellers, it is easier for a company to control prices and to exploit the consumer.

Public policy toward horizontal mergers has resulted in undoing some mergers and blocking others, as well as in deterring many mergers that might otherwise have occurred. As a result, it has not only prevented merger-induced increases in market concentration in many industries, but has also opened opportunities for deconcentration in other industries. A case study of the steel industry illustrates how amended Section 7 may affect industry structure.

Merger Policy and the Steel Industry

Prior to 1950, mergers had played a major role in creating and maintaining high market concentration in the United States steel industry. United States Steel, the dominant company in the industry, was a "consolidation of consolidations" comprising nearly 200 separate firms. Yet, as already noted, in 1920 the Supreme Court held that by making these mergers, United States Steel had not violated the Sherman Act. As recently as 1948 the Supreme Court sanctioned purchase of a competitor by United States Steel.[9] In addition, Bethlehem Steel Corporation, the country's second largest steel company, has attained much of its relative size through mergers (as have some other companies). It seems quite evident that the inability to attack mergers under the Sherman Act was largely responsible for the high level of concentration in the steel industry during the five decades prior to 1950.

It is especially significant, therefore, that one of the landmark cases brought under amended Section 7 involved the steel industry—the proposed merger in 1956 of Bethlehem Steel Corporation and Youngstown Sheet & Tube Company. This was the largest merger challenged under the new act. When the case was brought to trial in 1958, Bethlehem and Youngstown had assets of $2,195 million and $660 million, respectively. Bethlehem was the country's second largest steel company, with 16.3 percent of industry ingot capacity, and Youngstown was the sixth largest steel company, with 4.6 percent of industry ingot capacity. Their respective market positions were larger in some products and in certain geographic markets.

The merger would have increased the top four companies' share of industry ingot capacity from 59 percent to 64 percent. This figure would have been higher than in nearly any period since the formation of United States Steel in 1901.

One of the defenses of the proposed merger presented by Bethlehem and Youngstown was that steel mills in the Chicago area lacked sufficient capacity to satisfy demand in the area. As Judge Weinfeld put it, "Each defendant in urging the merger takes a dim view of its ability to undertake, on its own, a program to meet the existing and anticipated demand for heavy

[9] *U.S.* v. *Columbia Steel Co.*, 334 U.S. 495 (1948).

structural shapes and plates in the Chicago area." Judge Weinfeld rejected these arguments, which he interpreted as "matters of preference" more than matters of necessity.

In finding the proposed merger in violation of Section 7, Judge Weinfeld expressed the view that if this merger was permitted, it might well set off "a chain reaction of further mergers by the other but less powerful companies in the steel industry." The defendants also argued that the merger would enable Bethlehem-Youngstown to challenge the dominant position of United States Steel. Judge Weinfeld reasoned that if this was a sufficient defense to the merger, "then the remaining larger producers in the 'Big 12' could with equal logic urge that they, too, be permitted to join forces and to concentrate their economic resources in order to give more effective competition to the enhanced 'Big 2'; and so we reach a point of more intense concentration in an industry already highly concentrated—indeed we head in the direction of triopoly."

Subsequent events proved the wisdom of Judge Weinfeld's decision. After the merger was enjoined, both companies greatly expanded their capacity in the Chicago area. On December 3, 1962, Bethlehem announced plans to construct a steel plant at Burns Harbor, Indiana, thirty miles east of Chicago. By 1964 this plant was producing steel plates; subsequent expansion permitted production of cold rolled sheets and hot rolled sheets. The company plans to make the Burns Harbor plant into a completely integrated facility like its Sparrows Point plant. Between 1959 and 1965, Bethlehem increased its net investment in plant and property by nearly 50 percent—from $909 million to $1,334 million. Between 1959 and 1965 Youngstown expanded its net plant and property investment by one-third—from $330 million to $441 million.

The blocking of the Bethlehem-Youngstown merger had a clear effect on the structure of the steel industry. Between 1954 and 1963, concentration of shipments among the steel companies actually declined. Whereas in 1954 the top four companies accounted for 55 percent of the value added by "blast furnaces and steel mills" their share had dropped to 50 percent by 1963;

this is almost identical to the market share of Youngstown. Consequently, if the merger had been permitted, concentration would almost certainly not have declined. In fact, had this decision laid down a rule of law permitting a horizontal merger of this magnitude, it is highly probable that Judge Weinfeld's "chain reaction" theory would have become a reality, which would have greatly increased concentration.

Overall Impact of Merger Policy

The above example illustrates the process by which public policy may affect mergers in particular industries. If this example is representative of the overall impact of merger policy, it would be expected that the policy would have prevented increases in concentration not based on economies of large scale. Moreover, the high levels of concentration found in many industries are not based on technological imperatives. Hence, in the absence of mergers and other restrictions on competition, a general decline in concentration might be predicted.

Postwar market concentration trends support this hypothesis. Since 1947 there has been a pronounced downward trend in market concentration in many producer goods industries, particularly in highly concentrated ones. (See Chapter 3.) Upward movements in concentration have been most noticeable in consumer goods industries, where advantages of large-scale advertising and promotion are most pronounced. Although horizontal merger policy has reduced the growth of market concentration in the consumer goods industries, this policy alone does not offer a solution to the problem. As will be seen shortly, conglomerate merger policy may have some impact on this problem.

Public Policy toward Conglomerate Mergers

In recent years 70 percent or more of all large mergers have been so-called conglomerate mergers; that is, the merging companies were neither direct competitors nor customers of one another.

Public policy toward such mergers is still in the embryonic stage. Although, to date, the Supreme Court has found only two such mergers in violation of Section 7, these cases illustrate the way conglomerate mergers may injure competition.

The first Supreme Court decision (1964) involved the Consolidated Foods Corporation acquisition of Gentry, Incorporated, a seasoning manufacturer. Consolidated Foods, a large food wholesaler and retailer, purchased products from food manufacturers (for example, canners) that were potential buyers of Gentry products. This situation enabled Consolidated to engage in reciprocal selling—"I'll buy from you if you'll buy from me."

This practice can have serious anticompetitive effects when some competitors can practice it at the expense of their rivals (see Chapter 6). This was the case in the Consolidated-Gentry merger, because none of Gentry's competitors could practice reciprocal selling. As a result, Consolidated-Gentry achieved

> the power to foreclose competition from a substantial share of the markets for dehydrated onion and garlic, thereby jeopardizing the competitive opportunities of its small, relatively undiversified competitors and tending to lend further rigidity to an already heavily concentrated industry and to discourage the entry of new competitors.

The Supreme Court concluded that the reciprocity opportunities created by this merger resulted in "an irrelevant and alien factor intruding . . . into the choice among competing products."

The Supreme Court handed down its second, and most important, conglomerate merger decision in 1967 when it found that the Procter & Gamble Company's acquisition of the Clorox Chemical Company was in violation of the Celler-Kefauver Act. The merging companies were not direct competitors—P & G was the country's leading soap and detergent manufacturer, and Clorox was the country's leading manufacturer of household liquid bleach. At the time of the merger, P & G had sales of $1,156 billion and Clorox had sales of $40 million. The bleach industry was already highly concentrated—Clorox held about 50 percent of sales and the top four companies held 74 percent.

Before acquiring Clorox, P & G had analyzed the feasibility and desirability of entering the bleach industry. Although its experience in other household fields demonstrated that it had the capacity to enter the industry by 'building in," P & G decided that it would be preferable to enter by acquiring Clorox. It subsequently acquired Clorox for $30.3 million, which was far in excess of its tangible assets of $12.6 million.

By acquiring Clorox, P & G transformed the structure of the bleach industry. P & G was many times larger than Clorox, and its advertising budget alone was twice the total sales of Clorox. Because of its vast size and its strong market positions in the soap and detergent field, it had important competitive advantages over other bleach producers. For example, because of its overall promotional budget, it received discounts ranging from 20 percent to 30 percent or more in its magazine and television advertising. These were far greater than the discounts available to even the largest independent bleach company, the Purex Corporation, which had about 15 percent of the market. In addition, P & G's vast resources and strong position in other fields enabled it to engage in programs of subsidized expansion and highly costly promotional strategies that weakened its competitors. The record contains vivid examples of such practices.

The Supreme Court identified three ways in which the merger had altered the structure of the household liquid bleach industry. The substitution of Proctor & Gamble for Clorox (1) raised the entry barriers facing potential new competitors, (2) dissuaded existing smaller competitors from competing aggressively, and (3) eliminated P & G as a leading potential entrant into the liquid bleach industry. The merger's impact on entry barriers and its elimination of P & G as a potential entrant were considered anticompetitive because the bleach industry was already highly concentrated prior to the acquisition. Because of this, increasing the height of entry barriers and eliminating the leading potential competitor tended to affect adversely the structure of the bleach industry. Simply put, the merger promised to make an already poorly structured market worse.

The Consolidated Foods and the Proctor & Gamble cases illustrate how conglomerate mergers may injure competition and violate the Celler-Kefauver Act. To date, however, public policy in this area remains relatively uncharted. The ultimate direction of policy toward such mergers will set the tempo of conglomerate merger activity and the kinds of industrial organization in the decades ahead.

Future Course of Merger Activity

In each year since 1960 new merger records have been set, and should the frenzied activity of 1968 continue for several more years, much of American industry could irrevocably pass into the control of a relatively few corporate hands. It has been seen how public policy has virtually stopped mergers among direct competitors and has played a central role in preventing the emergence of hard-core oligopolies in many industries. But public policy has been less effective in dealing with the problems posed by conglomerate mergers.

The ultimate economic consequences of many contemporary conglomerate mergers are impossible to assess. Viewed in isolation, individual conglomerate mergers may seem to have little or no direct impact on competition. But the ultimate consequences of hundreds of such mergers will be to centralize further the control of United States industry among a few hundred corporations.

It has already been noted that the top 200 corporations expanded substantially their share of American industry since World War II. There is strong evidence, however, that if these concerns were forced to rely on internal growth rather than merger, not only would they have been unable to expand their relative position, but they would also have lost relative position over time. Hence, the growing aggregate concentration of American industry has not been built on economic imperatives. Many great conglomerates are rooted in the financial wizardry of their promoters rather than in superior economic efficiency. Consequently, further aggrandizement of financial power achieved by conglomerate mergers can be prevented without loss of economic efficiency. There is persuasive evidence that many jerry-built conglomerates are less efficient than were the individual companies they absorbed.

Certainly one of the most pressing economic issues confronting the nation is whether or not to bridle the mounting conglomerate merger movement that threatens to centralize control over much of the economy in a few vast, conglomerate enterprises. A related issue is how best to assure that existing large conglomerates operate in the public interest. We return to these questions in Chapter 11.

PATTERNS OF ANTITRUST ENFORCEMENT

Few antitrust cases were brought in the early years following passage of the Sherman Act in 1890. President Theodore Roosevelt initiated a vigorous antitrust program resulting in the breaking up of a number of leading trusts of the day—petroleum, tobacco, and explosives. The number of Sherman Act complaints rose from eighteen during 1891 to 1900 to sixty-three during 1901 to 1910. The number of enforcements expanded modestly over the next decade, but then declined during the 1920s.

The slow pace of early enforcement largely reflected the meager resources devoted to this purpose. In the first years following its creation in 1903, the Antitrust Division budget averaged only $100,000, and in no year prior to 1935 did its budget exceed $300,000. Under President Theodore Roosevelt the Antitrust Division had five attorneys and four stenographers.

A vigorous antitrust effort got under way in 1938 when President Franklin D. Roosevelt appointed Thurman Arnold as head of the Antitrust Division. Between 1938 and 1942 the division's budget increased from $413,394 to $2,325,000. This growth resulted in a vastly expanded enforcement effort. Whereas only eighty-three cases were brought under the Sherman Act during 1929–1938, over 500 cases were brought during the following decade. This was greater than during the entire preceding forty-eight years. Since World War II, the number of Sherman Act cases has continued high—over 400 during the ten-year period 1950–1959 and over 300 during the seven-year period 1960–1966. In the two latter periods the Department of Justice brought an additional fifty-two and 138 cases, respectively, under the Clayton Act.

The number of cases initiated by the Federal Trade Commission has also increased through the years. During 1960–1966 the commission initiated over 700 antimonopoly cases, plus numerous cases involving consumer protection matters, particularly in deceptive and misleading advertising.

In recent years the commission has placed increasing emphasis on various voluntary compliance programs designed to clarify, insofar as possible, the various laws enforced by it. The commission attempts to provide such guidance in a variety of ways, ranging from advisory opinions, given only on the request of an interested party, to trade regulation rules, representing conclusions of the commission and arrived at after appropriate hearings, about the illegality of particular practices. These various programs are based on one of the original arguments for the creation of FTC—"that businessmen desire something more than the menace of legal process."

Surprisingly, few contemporary commentators appreciate the massive nature of current antitrust enforcement efforts, particularly in relation to mergers. Indeed, the conventional wisdom among popular writers of various ideological persuasions is that antitrust is dead. (See Chapter 10.) Antitrust may be "dead" as a popular movement; yet it has seldom been more alive as a vigorous instrument of economic policy. Such a paradox requires the perspective of the historian. Richard Hofstadter has observed: "Despite the collapse of antitrust feeling both in the public at large and among liberal intellectuals, antitrust as a legal-administrative enterprise has been solidly institutionalized in the past quarter of a century." [9]

The year 1938 marked the beginning of this institutionalization process. In that year public policy turned sharply away from a system of planning rooted in government-sponsored cartelization of business, particularly as represented by the NRA, toward a policy relying primarily on competitive market forces.[10] In 1938, President Franklin D. Roosevelt, deeply disturbed by the 1937 recession, called for the creation of the Temporary National Economic Committee (TNEC), composed of members of both legislative chambers and officials of the executive branch. Although TNEC was viewed by its critics as an attack on the capitalist system itself, its chief goal was to learn more about the anatomy of twentieth-century capitalism. The inquiry focused on how the system worked and what might be done to make it work better. The chairman of the Federal Trade Commission and the Assistant Attorney General for Antitrust of the Department of Justice were among the members of TNEC. The committee necessarily relied heavily

[9] "What Happened to the Antitrust Movement?" in Earl F. Cheit (ed.), *The Business Establishment* (New York: Wiley, 1964), p. 116.

[10] In his autobiography Thurman Arnold points out that this decision was not kindly received by many liberals of the day. As he put it, "There was a belief among liberals at the time that the age of competition had gone and the age of planning had come." Thurman Arnold, *Fair Fights and Foul* (New York: Harcourt, Brace & World, 1965), p. 138.

upon the expertise of the professional staffs of the antitrust agencies. The reliance on such experts, of course, could not help but elevate the status of the agencies vis-à-vis the Congress and the public.

President Franklin D. Roosevelt's message urging the creation of the TNEC also called for a strengthening of antitrust enforcement. As already noted, the appointment of Thurman Arnold in 1938 ushered in what many have viewed as the golden era of antitrust, 1938–1943. Perhaps the main legacy of Arnold's reign, however, was not his big cases, but the demonstration that antitrust still had a meaningful role in a modern economy. As a result, even though antitrust enforcement was partially demobilized during World War II, the antitrust agencies rebounded strongly at the war's end, and the big cases went forward. Though considerably diminished in the eyes of the general public, an antitrust movement still stalked Washington in the immediate postwar years. Politicians and government officials schooled by the TNEC and the antitrust revival pushed for stronger antitrust laws, particularly for a new antimerger statute. It was this environment which made it possible to enact the Celler-Kefauver Act of 1950, which provided a powerful weapon against anticompetitive horizontal and vertical mergers, as mentioned earlier. The passage of the act might well be viewed as the capstone of the antitrust revival initiated more than a decade earlier. The passage of the new antimerger statute coincided roughly with the close of the antitrust movement.

The antitrust movement itself, however, left in its wake an essentially bipartisan consensus that antitrust enforcement was an indispensable, though an unpopular, instrument of public policy in the mid-twentieth century. This institutionalization process gave antitrust a secure berth in national policy. Thus, while a popular antitrust movement no longer exists, none is needed to sustain an effective antitrust program. There is no guarantee, of course, that the program will be adequate. But as Richard Hofstadter has concluded: "Once the United States had an antitrust movement without antitrust prosecutions; in our time there have been antitrust prosecutions without an antitrust movement." [11]

This bit of history explains why, in a sense, it was a historical imperative that the antitrust agencies respond as they did when the current merger movement began accelerating in 1954–1955. In 1950 Congress gave the agencies a mandate to prevent anticompetitive mergers; and the institutionalization process gave the agencies the capacity to carry out the mandate to a degree not otherwise possible. Consequently, long before the public even became aware of the dimensions of the current merger movement, the agencies began what resulted in the largest and most sustained antitrust effort in our history. This effort has faltered in recent years, however, as the merger movement has taken on an increasingly conglomerate character. Although the antitrust agencies, encouraged by favorable Supreme Court decisions, have explored cautiously the outer boundaries of the merger law, the efforts taken to date have not perceptibly slowed the pace of conglomerate merger activity threatening to irrevocably reshape the American economy. This experience demonstrates, perhaps, that institutionalized antitrust cannot be relied upon to meet dramatic new changes. *In times of crisis the nation once again needs an antitrust movement*.

American experience demonstrates that antitrust policy has played a central role in maintaining effective competition in the greater part of the economy. In recent years, however, antitrust has come under increasing attacks, from both the political left and the political right. The central issue, as will be seen in the next chapter, is whether Americans wish to substitute more extensive public planning and regulation for competitive market forces.

[11] *Op. cit.*, p. 114.

CHAPTER 10

The New Industrial
State

GALBRAITH THESIS

John Kenneth Galbraith has written a most provocative book entitled *The New Industrial State*.[1] In it Galbraith sets forth his conception of modern American capitalism. The Galbraith book has special relevance to this book, because it challenges many basic premises of a market-oriented economic system. If Galbraith is right, competitive capitalism is obsolete.

The heart of Galbraith's thesis is that over the past seventy-five years certain "technological imperatives" have wrought great changes in the basic arrangement of modern economic life, the ultimate consequence of which is the "diminished effectiveness of the market." As a result, "the market is replaced by planning."

Galbraith argues that modern technological imperatives make the vast, "mature" industrial enterprise a perfect mechanism for planning the invention, innovation, and production

[1] *The New Industrial State* (Boston: Houghton Mifflin, 1967). Galbraith capsuled his views in six Reith lectures delivered over the British Broadcasting Corporation and reproduced in *The Listener*.

processes. But market power is not only an end result; it is prerequisite to the success of the system. The requirements of large-scale production, heavy capital commitments, and sophisticated technology demand elaborate planning. Successful planning, in turn, requires management of consumer wants to suit the needs of the business enterprise. The planning process is carried on by what Galbraith labels, "the technostructure," which encompasses all the technicians and professionals required for effective group decision making.

Additionally, modern technology requires increasing participation in the planning process by the state, as many jobs are too big even for the largest private industrial complex. Finally, Galbraith believes that public policy aimed at maintaining competition is based on a nineteenth-century conception of the economy. He would therefore abandon our traditional policy of relying on market forces to limit and discipline the use of private economic market power.

Where is the new industrial state taking us? Galbraith predicts that the mature corporation is increasingly becoming a part of the administrative complex of the state and that the capitalist and the communist societies will gradually converge.[2] What will be the quality of life in the new industrial state? If we continue to subordinate all to material welfare, that is what we will get. On the other hand, if we raise our sights to more aesthetic goals, the industrial system will become "responsive to the larger purposes of society." Galbraith has shown "wherein the chance for salvation lies."[3] So, in the end, it will be up to us to choose. (This is a surprise ending in view of the irrepressible economic determinism that led to all Galbraith's earlier conclusions.)

Most economists will agree with much in Galbraith's "new industrial state." In fact, a great deal of what Galbraith says has become a part of the accepted economic wisdom—in 1932 Berle and Means first articulated the thesis of separation

[2] *Op. cit.*, pp. 389 ff.
[3] *Ibid.*, p. 399.

of business ownership and control.[4] But Galbraith has put together these and other old ideas—some accepted and some rejected by economists—into a new and bigger package. As always, when Galbraith goes over even familiar ground, he discovers new things and paints a different and grander landscape than his forebears. But as one not so friendly reviewer observed, "novelty isn't everything: one can make a decent case for the proposition that it is more important to be right then different."

Galbraith has articulated a provocative thesis concerning the causes and implications of "the new industrial state." Space permits analysis of only his key points:

1. Technological imperatives dictate vast industrial concerns and high levels of market concentration and, hence, the death of the market.
2. Public policy aimed at maintaining a market economy has failed in the past and is doomed to fail in the future.
3. The necessity for state planning in certain areas further diminishes the need for reliance on the market as a regulating and planning agent.

TECHNOLOGICAL IMPERATIVES

Most fundamental to the Galbraith thesis are the so-called technological imperatives that he views as the root causes of modern industrial organization. Galbraith asserts that we must have very large industrial complexes and high market concentration because of the requirements of large-scale production, invention, and innovation. As he puts it, "The enemy of the market is not ideology but technology." But what are the facts on this point?

[4] Adolf A. Berle and Gardiner C. Means, *The Modern Corporation and Private Property* (New York: Macmillan, 1932).

Recent studies of this subject are almost unanimous in con-cluding that productive efficiency dictates high concentration in only a small and declining share of all manufacturing in-dustries. On this point, there seems to be little disagreement.

The growing body of research into the extent to which large-scale economies dictate large business enterprise and high mar-ket concentration has already been discussed. The evidence is sharpest in productive efficiency—an especially crucial area, because of the public policy dilemma posed by industries with increasing returns to large scale. In clear-cut cases where large-scale production dictates monopoly, as with telephone and electric power, the United States answer has been either reg-ulation or government ownership. But, if such industries prove the rule rather than the exception, a basic question is raised about the compatibility of productive efficiency and a competi-tively structured economy. It is therefore extremely significant that recent studies are unanimous in concluding that produc-tive efficiency dictates high concentration in only a small—and declining—share of all manufacturing industries (see Chapter 4).

Galbraith does not, however, rest his case solely on the re-quirement of large-scale production. He further argues that economies of scale in research and innovation make high con-centration and near monopoly an inevitable consequence of modern capitalism. Since Joseph Schumpeter first set forth this doctrine in 1942 and Galbraith expanded on it in 1952,[5] it has been subjected to extensive empirical testing. But this matter has already been discussed, and the evidence shows that the theory has no general validity in explaining inventive and in-novative activity in American experience.

There simply is not persuasive evidence to support Gal-braith's thesis that, as a rule, vast size and market power are essential to successful innovation and planning. On this point his use of illustration betrays his case. Galbraith shows the matchless capability of the vast enterprise in planning, inven-

[5] John Kenneth Galbraith, *American Capitalism, The Concept of Coun-tervailing Power* (Boston: Houghton Mifflin, 1952), p. 91.

tive, and innovative activities by a hypothetical example of
how General Electric would go about the conception and birth
of a new pop-up toaster.

> The central characteristics of modern industry are illustrated
> by this culturally exciting invention. It would require a large
> organization, embracing many specialists, to get this product
> to consumers. Considerable capital would be required. While
> it is conceivably open to an individual entrepreneur, such as
> myself, to have an inspiration, no one would expect a one-man
> firm to produce such a product. It could be floated only by a
> big firm. All decisions on the toaster—those involving initia-
> tion, development, and ultimate acceptance or rejection—are
> the work of teams of specialists and are exercised deep down
> in the company. And no one would think of leaving price or
> demand to the market. The price would be subject to careful
> advance calculation. . . .[6]

Insight into this process is revealed better by experience
than by hypothetical example. What experience supports the
prediction that vast size is prerequisite to the development and
introduction of new products and processes? Let us first consider the electrical home appliances sold by General Electric.
Perhaps the past is prologue.

The electric toaster was not invented or introduced by a
great corporation such as General Electric, which would fit so
nicely Galbraith's invention-innovation-planning framework.
On the contrary, according to the late T. K. Quinn, vice-president of General Electric, it was developed and brought into
the market by a relatively small firm, the McGraw Company.
And, according to Quinn, "For many years none of the giant
companies were able to come near to matching [McGraw's]
toaster." [7] This is no exception. Quinn credited small companies with discovery and initial production of electric ranges,
electric refrigerators, electric dryers, electric dishwashers, the

---

[6] Second Reith lecture, p. 754. Galbraith also uses this illustration in
The New Industrial State, pp. 68–69.

[7] T. K. Quinn, *Giant Business* (New York: Exposition Press, 1953), p.
117.

hermetically sealed compressor, vacuum cleaners, clotheswashing machines, deep freezers, electric hot irons, and electric steam irons.[8] Indeed, Quinn summarized his own experience with GE:

> I know of no original product invention, not even electric shavers or hearing aids, made by any of the giant laboratories or corporations, with the possible exception of the household garbage grinder, developed not by the research laboratory but by the engineering department of General Electric. But the basic idea of this machine came from a smaller concern producing commercial grinders.[9]

Quinn concluded: "The record of the giants is one of moving in, buying out, and absorbing the smaller concerns."

Nor is this record unique to household appliances. In many other industries smaller companies generate at least their proportionate share of inventions and innovations, and they frequently do a good deal better than the industrial giants (see Chapter 4).

Perhaps Galbraith's "technological imperatives" assumption has greater validity in areas where invention and innovation costs are higher and the planning horizons are more distinct than they are in consumer goods products. Here, too, Galbraith's premises are based more on sands of fancy than rocks of evidence. Perhaps no industry fits so snugly the Galbraith model for ideal planning as does the United States steel industry. Since the creation of United States Steel in 1901, the American steel industry has been highly concentrated and dominated by big enterprises. Presumably this market structure provided what Galbraith views as the "prime requirement" of planning: "control over decision."

There can be no doubt that the market structure of the industry gave big steel considerable discretion in planning. But the relevant question is whether this discretion was used, as Galbraith's theory predicts. Fortunately in this case we need

8 *Ibid.*, pp. 116–117.
9 *Ibid.*, p. 177.

not rely on speculation. The leading steel companies clearly had a lackluster record as inventive and innovative forces in this most basic industry. The accomplishments of United States Steel have been especially disappointing. After an exhaustive study of the corporation, an engineering consulting firm reported to United States Steel in 1939 that it was lagging badly in many respects.[10] Nor has United States Steel or other large steel companies performed much better since 1939. A study of the thirteen major innovations in the American steel industry between 1940 and 1955 reveals that none was the outgrowth of American steel companies.[11] Four were based on inventions of European steel companies (generally small by American standards), and seven came from independent inventors.

Does Galbraith really want more industries structured like the United States steel industry? Would he have permitted this industry to become even more concentrated through mergers among small enterprises (for example, Bethlehem and Youngstown, discussed in Chapter 9) so that they could better emulate the performance of United States Steel?

IS THE MARKET DEAD?

As a corollary of his assumptions concerning technology, Galbraith argues that we can no longer rely on market forces to allocate resources. Because of this, he continues, the struggle to keep competition alive "has obviously been a losing one. Indeed, it has been lost." These assertions go to the heart of Galbraith's thesis: because the market has perished, we must be

[10] George W. Stocking, *Basing Point Pricing and Regional Development* (Chapel Hill, N.C.: University of North Carolina Press, 1954), p. 140.

[11] A study by Edwin Mansfield found that the leading steel companies also lagged in the innovation process. Edwin Mansfield, "Size of Firm, Market Structure, and Innovation," *Journal of Political Economics* (December 1963), pp. 556–576.

saved by extensive extra market planning. If this premise should prove faulty, Galbraith's thesis comes tumbling down.

It has already been seen that the evidence does not support Galbraith's thesis that as a general rule technological imperatives require high levels of industrial concentration. It should therefore come as no surprise that in many industries competitive forces are much stronger than Galbraith suggests, and that in many industries where concentration is highest, the market position of industry leaders is being eroded. It was noted earlier in the text that during the postwar years—between 1947 and 1966—market concentration tended to decline across a broad front in the producer goods sector of manufacturing. While this situation is in direct conflict with the predictions of Galbraith's thesis, it is entirely consistent with the empirical evidence referred to. Although in some industries technology may make it impossible for very small companies to operate efficiently, it does not dictate mammoth size and high levels of market concentration. Most American markets have become so large that they can sustain many efficient-sized enterprises.

Surprisingly, it is in consumer goods manufacturing industries that concentration has been on the rise in the postwar years. Of course, technological requirements in these industries demand relatively smaller enterprises than in producer goods manufacturing. The reasons for increasing concentration in consumer goods manufacturing are to be found in the requirements of product differentiation (especially the costs of large-scale promotion) and distribution, not in the technological imperatives that Galbraith assumes to be the kingpins of market power.

Postwar concentration trends viewed together with the recent findings concerning the relationship between technology and industrial organization provide a valuable insight into the future potential viability of the market as a regulator and planner of economic activity. Modern technology has not made obsolete the competitive, market-oriented economy of the United States. It is precisely in the producer goods manufacturing industries that economies of large-scale invention, innovation, production, and planning requirements are most pronounced. Yet many of these industries have experienced a significant drop in market concentration; it has occurred because many industrial markets have grown more rapidly than have the requirements of large-scale business organization.

These trends in market concentration may still be irrelevant if Galbraith's concept of market power is correct. Throughout his discussion he implies that, "characteristically," American industries are concentrated "oligopolies," and that the companies operating in them have great discretionary pricing power independent of the market. Galbraith is in serious error on two counts: (1) he is mistaken about the level and the trends of market concentration, and (2) he exaggerates the power of oligopolists.

In the first place, Galbraith not only wrongly implies that market concentration is increasing because of technological imperatives, but also overstates the levels of market concentration. In his book he says, "in the characteristic market of the industrial system there are only a handful of sellers." He then lists the automobile and seventeen other industries, stating that there are a "host" of others.[12] Galbraith has not selected a "characteristic" group of industries. (In each industry cited the top four did two-thirds or more of the business.) Of the "host" of other industries not cited, more than three out of four had lower levels of concentration. Also, thirteen of the eighteen high-concentration industries cited by Galbraith experienced declines in concentration in recent years. The big exceptions were consumer goods items—most notably automobiles, a favorite example of Galbraith.

Second, like Gertrude Stein, Galbraith has difficulties with shades of difference. Fortunately, however, all oligopolies are not alike, and there are important differences in the amount of market power conferred by varying market structures. The accumulating evidence of the relation between an industry's structure and its performance leaves little room for agnosticism about the powerful role played by the market in limiting dis-

[12] *The New Industrial State,* pp. 180–181.

cretionary pricing power (see Chapter 6). And, importantly, there is now persuasive evidence that in the larger part of American manufacturing industry, market forces limit quite severely the discretionary pricing power of companies. But again Galbraith has ignored the mounting evidence that runs counter to one of his central premises.[13]

These comments do not imply that strong positions of power are not entrenched in our economy—they are. Again, Galbraith greatly overstates his case. Importantly, however, whereas he pays tribute to companies with substantial market power—he believes such power is essential—the evidence indicates that companies with great power perform less admirably than he assumes. Hence, the facts support a public policy precisely opposite to that advocated by Galbraith—more competition is needed, not less. (Whether or not this is feasible shall be considered shortly.)

At first the rising concentration in consumer goods industries seems to bear out Galbraith's thesis that consumer wants should be managed to suit the needs of the business enterprise. But the causes of developments here are not rooted in Galbraith's technological imperatives. The requirements of large-scale production, invention, and innovation are less demanding in the manufacture of consumer goods than they are in other areas of manufacturing. It is true that many sellers try to manage consumer wants—but only because of the nature of competition where opportunities for product differentiation exist. True, the market operates less perfectly as a result—though the author suspects it operates better than Galbraith assumes. If Americans are really dissatisfied they can do something about this problem; but they probably will not. Nor does Galbraith recommend solutions for this knotty problem.

Despite its shortcomings, particularly in some consumer goods, the market clearly has not disappeared as the key coordinating and integrating force in allocating resources in most

13 In his two chapters on "Prices in the Industrial System," Galbraith does not cite a single empirical study to support his assertions; *ibid.,* pp. 178–197.

of the economy. The evidence simply does not support the generalization that technological and planning imperatives have changed so drastically in recent years as to dictate the demise of the market. When one studies the entire industrial landscape, the emerging picture is not the one painted by Galbraith. Whereas he concedes his thesis does not encompass the entire economy, close inspection shows it captures only a small part of the real world.

Galbraith says that he is not concerned with "the world of the independent shopkeeper, farmer, shoe repairman, bookmaker, narcotics peddler, pizza merchant, streetwalker, and the car and dog laundries." He feels obliged to emphasize this point, because "One should always cherish his critics and protect them where possible from foolish error. The tendency of the mature corporation in the modern industrial system to become part of the administrative complex of the state cannot be refuted by appeal to contrary tendencies elsewhere in the economy." But as shown earlier, Galbraith's thesis explains only a small part of the manufacturing sector of the economy. Moreover, his technological imperatives obviously are even less important in wholesale and retail trade, in the services industry, and in agriculture, which today comprise about 35 percent of national income outside the government sector. Nothing drastically new has occurred in the other segments of the economy that suggests a trend toward decreasing importance of market forces. Competition in transportation and finance, for example, industries that generate another 13 percent of national income, is probably more effective today than it was in prewar years. The remainder, communications and public utilities, provide another 5 percent of national income. But these, of course, have been subject to some degree of regulation since at least the 1930s.

IS ANTITRUST A CHARADE?

The mere absence of factors requiring high market concentration does not guarantee that excessive concentration will not arise or that it will decline in industries where it already is too high. Simply put, effective competition is not a plant that blooms unattended. Powerful companies may engage in competitive strategies that counteract the forces working toward deconcentration. Specifically, until the passage of the Celler-Kefauver Act in 1950, horizontal and vertical mergers often had the effect of offsetting these forces, with the result that in many industries concentration remained unchanged or even increased.

Again, however, Galbraith has neglected his homework. He has not kept abreast of contemporary policy or its effects. He asserts that it is a "charade" acted out, "not to prevent exploitation of the public" but "to persuade people in general and British Socialists and American liberals in particular, that the market is still extant." [14] He sums up his views of current antitrust policy: "A great corporation wielding vast power over its markets is substantially immune. . . . But if two small firms seek to unite, this corporate matrimony will be meticulously scrutinized. And, very possibly, it will be forbidden." [15]

These assertions simply do not square with the facts. Antimerger effort has been directed almost exclusively against the largest industrial concerns. It has not been, as Galbraith suggests, an attack on industrial midgets. Over 60 percent of the largest corporations, those with assets of over one billion dollars, and nearly a third of the top two hundred have been subjects of antimerger complaints. These complaints have challenged not miniscule mergers but rather mergers by large concerns. (This matter is discussed at length in Chapter 9.) This enforcement effort represents a great victory for competi-

[14] Third Reith lecture, p. 794.
[15] *Ibid.*

tion and clearly demonstrates that antitrust policy can be an effective instrument of public policy in the last half of the twentieth century.

It is true that antitrust policy cannot easily—and certainly not quickly—solve problems of deeply entrenched power. Fifty years of ineffective public policy toward mergers have resulted in unnecessarily high concentration in many industries. But recent developments show that much can be accomplished. Whether or not the market survives in the greater part of our economy, or is destroyed by vast aggregations of market power, will be determined not by technological and planning imperatives but by public policy toward the achievement and retention of power. The market may well be destroyed in the next generation, as Galbraith predicts, but not for his reasons. It will be a matter of public will or neglect, not technology.

PLANNING AND THE STATE

In the "new industrial state" the government plays a central role in economic planning, with a concomitant dimunition in reliance upon the market. Specifically, it stabilizes aggregate demand, underwrites expensive technology, restrains wages and prices to limit inflation, provides technical and educational manpower, and buys upwards of one-fifth of our economic output.

It is true that the government does these things, and more. But Galbraith exaggerates the role of the state (as opposed to the market) in the planning process.[16] He points out correctly

[16] He also is incorrect in implying that the great role of the state as a customer of goods and services is mainly related to technological imperatives. It is true that the state buys nearly one-fifth of our economic output. But what are these purchases? In 1967 expenditures related to our military and international commitments and the cost of past wars accounted for fully 79 percent of the federal budget: national defense (54 percent), space research and technology (5 percent), international affairs and finance (4

that one major responsibility of the modern state is to sustain aggregate demand and stimulate economic growth. He fails to perceive, however, that the state's planning in this respect is neither in competition with, nor a substitute for, planning by business enterprise, and such planning by the state certainly does not require abandonment of the market. On the contrary, the basic philosophy of the Employment Act of 1946 is that the state create a general economic environment within which private enterprise can generate economic growth (see Chapter 7). Within this environment the basic "planning" decisions of what to produce and how much of each product to produce are left to private enterprise responding to aggregate demand.

Experience increasingly demonstrates the heavy role played by the market in implementing or frustrating monetary and fiscal policy aimed at full employment. Only if competition is effective can extensive price controls be avoided as a necessary adjunct to planning for rapid economic growth without inflation (see Chapter 7).

The wage and price guideposts created by the Council of Economic Advisers under Presidents John F. Kennedy and Lyndon B. Johnson are a symptom of the absence of effective competition in some segments of the economy. But, happily, these segments are in the minority. Were it otherwise, it probably would be impossible to push to high employment without implementing extensive wage and price controls.

None appreciate these facts of life so keenly as those economists responsible for full-employment policy during 1961–68. Walter Heller, the former chairman of the Council of Economic Advisers and prime mover in gaining public acceptance for the "new economics," has emphasized the importance of keeping competition alive. He does not believe that planning for rapid economic growth requires abandonment of the market.

---

percent), veterans' benefits (5 percent), and interest on the national debt (11 percent). Thus the growing size of the federal budget is the outcome not of technological imperatives but of our growing military and international commitments.

Rather, in his recent book he argues forcibly that competition must be made more effective, not less.

> There are substantial differences among economists on how far the government should go in protecting consumers or setting guideposts for wages and prices. But there is little difference—at least among the vast majority of economists—in supporting strong measures to protect the free play of market forces against monopoly and price-fixing, and in strongly opposing direct wage and price controls as inefficient and inequitable substitutes for market forces, to be considered only as a last resort in a war economy.[17]

In a similar vein, the Joint Economic Committee of the Congress has repeatedly emphasized the importance of maintaining effectively competitive markets, and the author does not think they are merely playing charades. The committee's 1967 report on the Economic Report of the President concluded, "Antitrust must be assigned a central role in national economic policy of no less significance than monetary and fiscal policy."

One thing must be made clear. Many of the most pressing problems of the day—water and air pollution, job retraining, urban and rural poverty, preservation of natural resources, promotion of basic research, to name a few—certainly require action and planning by the state. But it is wrong to infer that the failure of the market to solve such problems represents a major flaw in the system. Unfortunately, many persons are inclined to damn the market—which to them means the businesses operating within it—for failing to do jobs better left to the state. Unfortunately, the defensively hostile responses of some business leaders to every social welfare proposal lend credence to the argument that the real issue at stake is the market system. Actually, however, the main issues usually are whether a particular job should be done at all and who is going to pay

17 Walter W. Heller, *New Dimensions of Political Economy* (New York: Norton, 1966), pp. 8–9.

for it. Once it is agreed that there is nothing inherently un-American or antimarket in the admission that some things are best left to the state, the state and the market can coexist in harmony. In truth, the one is the indispensable complement of the other; they are not rivals nor is one a substitute for the other.

CHAPTER 11

An Agenda to Promote Competition

Competition remains a powerful and pervasive force disciplining private economic power in the greater part of the economy. Nor have the requirements of modern technology made competitive capitalism obsolete. On the contrary, the opportunities for effective competition are greater today than in past decades. But the fact that technology permits a competitively structured economy does not guarantee that such an economy will continue to exist.

Various developments are underway tending to centralize corporate decision making among a relatively few vast, conglomerate enterprises. These developments are being propelled not by irrepressible economic imperatives, but by economic arrangements contrived by men. They are therefore also susceptible to social control. Simply put, market competition can be maintained—indeed, it can be increased—if Americans can develop a political consensus that places the maintenance of competition among key public policy goals.

Today, competitive capitalism faces not one but several threats to its very survival. This calls for immediate action.

Existing antitrust legislation is sufficient to deal with most of these threats; in some cases, however, additional legislation may be required. The agenda set forth below is not exhaustive. It focuses on priority areas. But if we cannot come to grips with these areas, matters not mentioned here may be of only academic interest.

SUPPORT FOR ANTITRUST ENFORCEMENT

Antitrust policy has never been given a fair test. The agencies given responsibility for enforcing this policy have never been adequately funded or staffed. Despite the growing complexity and size of the economy, the Federal Trade Commission and the Department of Justice have fewer than 1,500 employees to enforce the antitrust laws. This is less than one-third as many employees as the five hundredth largest industrial corporation. The vast array of legal forces defending a major antitrust complaint before the FTC or a district court far exceeds the representation of the government. The number of antitrust practitioners in the private bar also far exceeds the number of lawyers in the antitrust agencies.

Although the potential returns to the economy for vigorous antitrust enforcement are enormous, actual prosecution expenditures fall far short of even the direct payoff of enforcement. For example, prevention of a single price conspiracy may result in savings to consumers many times greater than the total tax revenue allotted to antitrust enforcement. Victims of the great electrical price conspiracy of the 1950s (see Chapter 9) received treble damage awards exceeding $500 million, which is greater than the total budget appropriations of the antitrust agencies over the eight decades of their existence. The indirect payoff of effective antitrust enforcement is many times greater than the measurable direct effects. The enforcement effort during the 1950s and 1960s against anticompetitive horizontal and vertical mergers virtually stopped all mergers of these types, thereby opening up opportunities for the deconcentration that occurred in many manufacturing industries between 1947 and 1966.

With adequate funding and staffing of antitrust agencies, there is, in most cases, no need for rewriting existing antitrust laws, as mentioned above. The Sherman, Clayton, and Federal Trade Commission Acts provide a broad and flexible basis for action. If vigorously and imaginatively enforced, these statutes are sufficient to cope with most of the chief threats to competition. Some of the areas detailed below, on the other hand, may require new legislation.

CONTROL OF CONGLOMERATE MERGERS

A vast and still accelerating conglomerate merger movement is sweeping across American industry. Although the ultimate effects of this movement are not apparent, it promises to further concentrate economic resources and private decision making in a relatively few conglomerate enterprises. Public action cannot await definitive answers to all the perplexing questions concerning the underlying causes and consequences of this movement. The stakes are too high to wait.

The movement is not being propelled by technological forces promising to improve the efficiency, productivity, and wealth of the nation. Rather, its mainspring consists of financial motivations that may benefit individual managers and stockholders, but do not promise a social dividend.

The ultimate effects of the growing centralization of economic power are not completely known. But American economic history teaches that highly centralized economic power holds within it a potential for creating serious social, political, and economic problems for a free society. A democratic society will not long tolerate great concentrations of undisciplined economic power. Such power is, however, especially vulnerable to attack. Centralized private power may for a time forestall efforts to control it, but ultimately such power will be subject either to direct social control—through administrative regulation—or to nationalization. Experience with both alternatives in democratic societies suggests that neither is preferable to the economic restraints of effective market competition. Neither can guarantee that the regulators will not become the servants of the very parties they are assigned to regulate. And experience shows that too often the rigid hand of private monopoly is replaced by the timid and unimaginative hand of bureaucracy.

Immediate steps should be taken to bridle the current merger movement, and this is one area where existing antitrust law may be inadequate for the task. Although to date over 800 mergers have been challenged under the Celler-Kefauver Act of 1950, this effort, restricted largely to horizontal and vertical mergers, has left largely untouched the great bulk of conglomerate mergers.

In the last year a series of bold steps has been taken to cope with accelerating conglomerate merger activity. The Federal Trade Commission and the Department of Justice have recently challenged a number of very large conglomerate mergers: Kennecott Copper Company's acquisition of Peabody Coal; White Consolidated's attempted takeover of Allis Chalmers; LTV's acquisition of Jones & Laughlin Steel Company; Northwest Industries attempted takeover of B. F. Goodrich Company; ITT's acquisition of Canteen Corporation; and ITT's proposed acquisition of Grinnell Corporation and Hartford Fire Insurance Company. In the spring of 1969, the FTC began requiring large corporations to report their mergers to the FTC sixty days prior to consummation, and to provide the agency with information that would permit the antitrust authorities to make more expeditious judgments concerning a merger's probable competitive effects. In addition, in 1969 Congress took its first serious look at the impact of the tax laws on growth by merger, although it failed to close some of the most egregious loopholes. Finally, in the fall of 1969 the House and Senate Antitrust subcommittees initiated extensive hearings into conglomerate mergers with a view to determining the need for new legislation.

This accelerating interest into the causes and consequences of the current merger movement is long overdue. Should the courts hold that the present antitrust laws are not adequate to cover recently challenged mergers, only new legislation will prevent the massive industrial reorganization that doubtless will follow such court decisions.

FULLER DISCLOSURE OF CONGLOMERATE OPERATIONS

Even if the current merger movement is brought under control through either expanded enforcement or new legislation, existing conglomerate enterprises may still threaten the ability of the market mechanism to discipline private economic power. Conglomerate enterprises may exercise economic power in subtle ways immune to existing forms of social control (see Chapter 6). The most promising approach to these problems is to make the operations of giant conglomerate enterprises more visible. A chief difficulty in identifying and measuring the significance of a particular conglomerate's conduct is that there is generally very little public information available about the financial characteristics of its constituent parts. The public financial statements of conglomerate enterprises are almost universally presented on a consolidated basis. This makes it virtually impossible to interpret the impact of particular business practices on profits. As one Wall Street analyst observed, "When you look at a conglomerate all you see is a smiling face; you don't know what it really looks like inside."

In a market economy heavy reliance is placed on the response of businessmen and investors to profit opportunities. Investors direct the flow of capital funds into the most efficient enterprises. But as a company becomes increasingly conglomerated, its public financial reports become less and less useful to investors. Each time another company is absorbed by a conglomerate, public knowledge of the private enterprise system is further diminished.

Moreover, a market economy relies heavily on the self-corrective mechanism of the market place to keep competition alive. When a company holds a strong market position resulting in high noncompetitive profits, the large profits act as a magnet inducing new entry. Or, conversely, when a company has unnecessarily high costs, a factor causing unprofitable operations, this condition too attracts entry and spurs competitors to better the inefficient company. But again the published financial satements of the conglomerate enterprise mask both the high profits and the high costs of its various operations.

The preceding problems could be largely corrected if the conglomerate enterprise were required to make detailed operating information available to the public, including sales and profits on a divisional basis or, where practical, a product basis. Some have argued that such fuller public reporting is not feasible, and that, even if feasible, the requirement represents an undesirable intrusion into the affairs of businessmen, a revealing of "trade secrets" to the public.

As for the first point, accountants will always disagree on what is practical. But no one can seriously argue with the proposition that it is possible to generate and make public much more detailed financial information than is presently the case.

The trade secrets objection is largely an artificial and a strained argument, since knowledge concerning sales and profits is necessary to intelligent decision making in a free enterprise economy. It is difficult to see how large conglomerate enterprises would be treated unfairly or injured by providing financial information when smaller, more specialized companies already provide such information.

The argument for disclosing conglomerate operations is neither new nor revolutionary. Ever since the states began granting corporate charters to private business, there have been laws requiring disclosure of company operations. In his first annual message to Congress in 1901, President Theodore Roosevelt made an eloquent statement setting forth the rationale underlying such disclosure. He assumed as self-evident the premise that "Great corporations exist only because they are created and safeguarded by our institutions; and it is therefore our right and our duty to see that they work in harmony with these institutions."

In Roosevelt's view, public accountability required extensive public information above all else: "The first requisite is knowledge, full and complete knowledge which may be made public to the world." He therefore concluded that steps should be taken to make public "full and accurate information" about the operations of the large corporations of the day.

No one seriously disputed the need for more public information concerning the "giant" corporations operating around the turn of the century. One result of this thinking was the creation of the Bureau of Corporations in 1903, which was merged into the Federal Trade Commission in 1914. Since that time additional steps have been taken periodically to require more public disclosure of private enterprise. A notable step was taken in 1934 when the Securities and Exchange Commission was created. But in recent decades public disclosure has not kept pace with the growing conglomeration of American business. Compared with the corporations of today, the corporate "giants" that troubled Theodore Roosevelt were midgets. As noted earlier, the three largest industrial corporations of today have greater combined sales than the total sales of all manufacturing enterprises in 1899. Quite clearly, unless the great conglomerate corporations are required to make a fuller public accounting of their operations, there can be no guarantee that they will operate in the interest of and in harmony with the institutions that create and protect them.

Although the SEC recently imposed fuller disclosure requirements on corporations, they fall short of the needed reform. Ironically, small corporations are required to report in fuller detail than are large corporations.

REDUCTION OF EXCESSIVE
MARKET POWER

Quite apart from the new problems posed by the conglomerate enterprise, market concentration is so high in a few strategic industries that management has considerable discretion over pricing and related decisions. Such discretionary power poses serious problems for programs aimed at achieving price stability, full employment, and rapid economic growth (see Chapter 7). It should be basic public policy, therefore, to improve the competitive behavior of industries holding such power.

Successful pursuit of such a policy does not require new legislation. A wide range of public policy instruments is already available, including the Sherman and Federal Trade-Commission Acts, plus such complementary measures as international trade policy, federal patent and licensing policies, government procurement and disposal policies, and government research and development policy. The postwar restructuring of the aluminum industry illustrates how several policies—in this case, antitrust, war plant disposal policies, and stockpile procurement policies (see Chapter 9)—may be used to restructure an industry.

This is not a proposal for widespread divestiture or dismemberment of numerous large corporations. Fortunately, massive industrial restructuring is not necessary to achieve important results. As noted earlier, the greater part of the American economy remains competitive and therefore is not in need of restructuring. Moreover, if a coordinated approach is pursued, wide scale divestiture is probably unnecessary even in industries posing the greatest problems. Finally, the problem that divestiture poses for a very large business has probably been greatly exaggerated in the past. The ease with which many enterprises have recently acquired, reorganized, and spun off huge portions of their assets suggests that restructuring business operations need not necessarily result in serious disruptions.

The business community should not view steps to reinvigorate competition as hostile attacks on big business. On the contrary, such actions should be viewed as therapy essential to the maintenance of competitive capitalism.

President Kennedy put the issue well when he said "There is no long-range hostility between business and the Government. There cannot be. We cannot succeed unless they succeed. But that doesn't mean we should not meet our responsibilities under antitrust . . ." [1]

BANK AND RAILROAD HOLDING COMPANIES

The recent creation of holding companies by the nation's largest banks and railroads for the purpose of entering other areas of business holds a potential for further centralization of corporate control (see Chapter 3). Federal Reserve Chairman William McChesney Martin has observed that in the case of banks this development "can affect the whole capitalistic system in the United States. The line between banking and commerce should not be erased."

This development not only promises to centralize corporate decision making over vast segments of the economy, thereby affecting competitive behavior in many subtle ways; it will also magnify the difficulties administrative agencies already face in effectively regulating banks and railroads. Additionally, there is danger that resources will be drained from railroad and bank operations, both of which are peculiarly related to the public interest, to finance growth in other areas. For these reasons steps should be taken immediately to contain this development, through new legislation if necessary.

[1] The President's News Conference, November 8, 1961, John F. Kennedy, *Public Papers of the President*, 1962, p. 708.

Chances appear good for enactment shortly of new legislation placing limitations on the expansion into nonbanking activities of bank holding companies. Banking interests are likely to be successful, however, in attempts to permit those banks that have already expanded outside of banking to keep their holdings.

LIMITATION OF CONTROL BY BANK TRUST DEPARTMENTS

A growing share of corporate securities is held in trust by commercial banks (see Chapter 3). Because trust departments typically have sole discretion in controlling such stock through voting, this development creates a new potential for control over other parts of the economy by banks. The result may be further centralization of corporate decision making. As with some other forces threatening to centralize economic power, we now only partially perceive the ultimate results of this development; but there is an immediate need for coming to grips with the problem. Public policy must be formulated to prevent this new potential for control for being exercised contrary to the public interest.

ELIMINATION OF CORPORATE MANAGEMENT INTERLOCKS

Section 8 of the Clayton Act of 1914 was enacted to prevent the lodging of control over decisions of particular industries in "a mere handful of men." Changes in industrial organization over the past half-century have rendered the provisions of Section 8 inadequate. It has been seen that the typical large conglomerate enterprise operates astride numerous industries. Consequently, even though two conglomerates may not be direct competitors today, they are potential competitors of one another, or they may meet in buyer-seller relationships. The interlocking of the corporate managements directing such businesses has a potential for reducing independent buyer-seller or expansion decisions. Such ties create an atmosphere for galvanizing what already may be a tendency for an accommodation of interests. Additionally, many large corporations, often in direct competition with one another, are indirectly interlocked through banks and insurance companies that have directors on the boards of numerous companies.

To minimize the opportunity for centralization of management decision making, large corporations should be prohibited from having either officers or directors on the boards of other large corporations, whether or not they are direct competitors. At the very least, indirect management interlocks should be prohibited where they link the managements of direct competitors.

PROMOTION OF INTERNATIONAL COMPETITION

International trade can exercise a powerful disciplining influence over domestic sellers with market power. International trade broadens the market beyond domestic boundaries and thus increases the number of sellers vying for the patronage of American buyers.

Recent steps toward freer trade are jeopardized on several fronts. Domestically, a number of important industries are seeking greater protection from foreign competition. On the other hand, sellers in foreign nations are forming export cartels in selling to the United States, sometimes with the blessing of American interests. Strong arguments have been advanced that such *voluntary* controls designed to limit exports to the United States are preferable to *mandatory* quotas limiting imports. There is the hope that the former will prove less enduring than the latter. Nonetheless, such arrangements should be explicitly recognized for what they are—international cartels created for the avowed purpose and intent of limiting exports to the United States. By limiting imports they almost surely raise prices to American consumers. Inherent in this approach is the probability that through a series of individual arrangements, large parts of international trade will become cartelized without any overall policy decisions ever having been made concerning the situation.

Another threat to freer international competition lies in the growing multinational character of the large modern corporation. Such corporations tend to lose their national identities and, perhaps, their national allegiances. This development makes it increasingly difficult for any one nation to exercise effective social control over international business operations. It is, therefore, imperative that the free nations seek a common solution to this problem, lest the accomplishments of the Kennedy round in dismantling public trade barriers be offset by the erection of privately constructed barriers.

CONSTITUENCY REQUIRED BY COMPETITIVE CAPITALISM

Market competition will not survive as an effective regulator of private decision making unless Americans develop a clearer vision of what can and must be done to maintain competition. We have seen that Galbraith is wrong. The market is not dead; nor do technological imperatives dictate that it will perish in this generation. Technology is not "the great enemy of the market," as Galbraith asserts; the enemy is neglect and lethargy on the part of its would-be friends—"liberals" and "conservatives" alike. Many liberals—including Galbraith—have apparently become disenchanted with the market because they feel it does not work well enough. Many conservatives, while professing great faith in the efficacy of the market, assiduously seek to shelter themselves from the competitive fray, whether through protective tariffs or special antitrust exemptions.

Unhappily, the future of competition is in doubt because it lacks a sufficiently broad-based constituency. The danger is that competitive capitalism may be abandoned without any clear notion of whether it will be replaced by a superior form of economic organization. Thoughtful Americans should recall what will be lost if market competition is allowed to die of neglect. Walter Adams and Horace M. Gray describe succinctly the values of an effectively competitive market system:

> We must realize that competition provides an effective technique for reconciling the dual objectives of economic welfare and economic freedom. It is a system which, if properly managed, enables men to maximize productivity and freedom simultaneously. It solves the production problem by mobilizing the talents and initiative of all men, not just a few, under the impartial direction of a free market and a free price system. It solves the power problem by diffusing power among all the participants in production so that each has enough power to produce but not enough to oppress others. In short, the rigorous discipline of the free market serves the twofold function of compelling efficiency and preventing exploitation.[2]

No one familiar with United States economic history is so naïve as to believe real world competition has ever worked as it does in the economist's model of perfect competition. Moreover, in some American industries today it is impossible to have effective competition under the best of circumstances.

But to recognize that the world is not perfectly round does not prove that it is flat. Nor does the absence of perfect competition prove the presence of monopoly. There is now rich empirical evidence demonstrating that market behavior of even large enterprises becomes severely restrained when market concentration is moderate and where entry is not seriously impeded. There also is clear-cut evidence that over the past

[2] *Monopoly in America* (New York: Macmillan, 1955), p. 177.

fifteen years market concentration has declined in many producer goods industries. Finally, there is persuasive evidence that in the greater part of American industry technological imperatives do not dictate the development of high market concentration.

The last point has important implications for the kind of economic system possible in 1975 or in 2000, if we wish to take the necessary steps to make it so. Simply put, considering technological requirements alone, the opportunities for effective competition in many parts of the economy are greater today than they were in 1890, the year the Sherman Antitrust Act was passed.

This is not to imply, of course, that the market can or should be relied upon to perform all economic functions. The market cannot be relied upon to solve a broad range of problems automatically. Some problems will yield only to public action. But recognition of this fact is not an argument for abandonment of reliance on competitive market forces as a planner and regulator of economic activity in other areas. On the contrary, whenever the government assumes a new responsibility, the more essential it becomes that as much of the economy as possible is regulated by the market rather than by the government. Wherever the market system works effectively, it is possible to avoid government intervention into the economically and politically hazardous thicket of specifying complex dimensions of economic performance.

American experience in various areas of business regulation, for example, in transportation and communications, demonstrates conclusively the great economic and political difficulties inherent in the regulatory process. In view of our regulatory experience in even such simple industries as transportation, it is alarming to imagine the extension of direct regulation to more complex sectors of the economy. Yet such an extension is surely the only alternative if market competition is allowed to wither. If control of American industry should become lodged in only a few hands, the American answer will almost certainly be the extension of governmental controls. Thus the ultimate organization of the American economic system will depend in a large part on whether or not the constituency of competitive capitalism can be enlarged. In the end it will be public attitudes toward the competitive system, not "natural" economic laws, that determine its fate.

Appendix A / Tables

TABLE A1 / NUMBER OF MANUFACTURING AND MINING CONCERNS ACQUIRED, 1940–1967

Period	Number	Period	Number
1940	140	1954	387
1941	111	1955	683
1942	118	1956	673
1943	213	1957	585
1944	324	1958	589
1945	333	1959	835
1946	419	1960	844
1947	404	1961	954
1948	223	1962	853
1949	126	1963	861
1950	219	1964	854
1951	235	1965	1,008
1952	288	1966	995
1953	295	1967	1,496
		1968	2,442

SOURCE: Federal Trade Commission, *Staff Report on Corporate Mergers,* 1969.

TABLE A2 / MANUFACTURING AND MINING MERGERS, 1948–1968

Year	TOTAL LARGE ACQUISITIONS *		TOTAL ACQUIRED BY 200 LARGEST FIRMS	
	Number	Assets (millions)	Number	Assets (millions)
1948	6	$ 101	4	$ 65
1949	5	67	4	45
1950	4	173	1	20
1951	9	201	5	125
1952	14	338	6	176
1953	23	679	15	438
1954	35	1,426	16	916
1955	67	2,117	36	1,298
1956	55	1,991	34	1,486
1957	51	1,442	26	951
1958	37	1,077	21	755
1959	64	1,959	33	1,350
1960	62	1,708	32	1,043
1961	55	2,056	24	1,295
1962	72	2,174	34	1,312
1963	71	2,956	40	2,081
1964	89	2,707	41	1,378
1965	90	3,827	27	2,009
1966	99	4,167	36	2,470
1967	167	9,062	71	6,431
1968 †	201	12,800	88	8,257
Total	1,276	$53,025	594	$33,900

* Acquired units with assets of $10 million or more.
† Figures for 1968 are preliminary.

SOURCE: Federal Trade Commission, *Staff Report on Corporate Mergers,* 1969.

TABLE A3 / CHANGE IN CONCENTRATION BETWEEN 1947 AND 1966 IN 213 MANUFACTURING INDUSTRIES

A. Number of Industries

Type of industry	Number of industries	NUMBER OF INDUSTRIES IN WHICH 4-FIRM CONCENTRATION—			NUMBER OF INDUSTRIES IN WHICH 8-FIRM CONCENTRATION—		
		Increased 3 percentage points or more	*Changed less than 3 percentage points*	*Decreased 3 percentage points or more*	*Increased 3 percentage points or more*	*Changed less than 3 percentage points*	*Decreased 3 percentage points or more*
Total	213	88	47	78	97	52	63
Producer goods	132	41	31	60	47	36	48
Consumer goods	81	47	16	18	50	16	15
Undifferentiated	28	12	7	9	14	7	7
Moderately differentiated	36	21	9	6	22	8	6
Highly differentiated	17	14	0	3	14	1	2

B. Value of Shipments

	Industry shipments (millions)	*Percent distribution of shipments*			*Percent distribution of shipments*		
Total	$222,353	37%	20%	43%	41%	29%	30%
Producer goods	134,659	20	25	55	25	38	37
Consumer goods	87,694	63	11	26	65	16	19
Undifferentiated	14,197	29	15	56	25	16	59
Moderately differentiated	33,449	59	24	17	66	26	8
Highly differentiated	40,048	78	0	22	79	7	14

SOURCE: "Industrial Structure and Competition," in *Studies by the Staff of the Cabinet Committee on Price Stability* (January 1969), p. 59.

TABLE A4 / AVERAGE FOUR AND EIGHT FIRM CONCENTRATION
RATIOS BY TYPE OF INDUSTRY 1947–66

	213 Industries	*Producer goods*	CONSUMER GOODS, DEGREE OF DIFFERENTIATION			
			All	*Low*	*Mod.*	*High*
	Average four-firm concentration					
1966	41.9	43.4	39.6	25.9	40.5	60.2
1963	41.4	43.3	38.2	23.8	39.6	59.0
1958	40.2	43.1	35.5	22.0	37.3	54.7
1954	40.6	43.8	35.4	22.9	36.4	53.6
1947	41.2	45.1	34.8	25.0	36.0	48.2
Change, 1947–66	0.7	−1.7	4.8	0.9	4.5	12.0
	Average eight-firm concentration					
1966	55.2	57.4	51.7	36.5	53.3	73.1
1963	54.4	57.2	50.0	33.6	52.2	72.2
1958	53.0	56.8	47.0	30.9	49.7	68.5
1954	53.3	57.4	46.6	32.1	48.5	66.4
1947	53.3	57.7	46.2	34.8	48.1	60.9
Change, 1947–66	1.9	−0.3	5.5	1.7	5.2	12.2

SOURCE: "Industrial Structure and Competition Policy," in *Studies by the Staff of the Cabinet Committee on Price Stability* (January 1969), p. 58.

Appendix B / Summary of Major Antitrust Statutes[1]

SHERMAN ANTITRUST ACT OF 1890

Declares illegal (1) contracts, combinations or conspiracies in restraint of trade, (2) monopolizing, attempting to monopolize, combining or conspiring to monopolize trade. Contains a general exemption for vertical minimum resale price-maintenance agreements on identified commodities in free and open competition, when lawful as applied to intrastate transactions under the law of the place of resale.

The Attorney General may bring simultaneous civil and criminal suits against an offender based on the same misconduct, or he may bring the suits consecutively, or select the type of suit he desires to bring.

. . .

The act also provides that a private person who is injured in his business or property by reason of violation of the act may maintain an action for treble damages. The United States is not a "person" as the term is used in section 7 of the act and, therefore, may not recover an action for treble damages. . . . But [it has been held that] a state is a "person" within the meaning of section 7 of the act, and, therefore, [can] maintain an action for treble damages. The same is true for municipalities. . . .

1 These summaries are excerpts from *Congress and the Monopoly Problem* (Washington, D.C.: U.S. House of Representatives, Select Committee on Small Business, 89th Cong., 2d Sess., 1966), pp. 129–130, 134–137.

FEDERAL TRADE COMMISSION ACT

Prevention of Unfair Competition

Under section 5 of the Federal Trade Commission Act, the Commission is charged with preventing unfair methods of competition and unfair or deceptive acts or practices in commerce, in the interest of the public. In connection with this function, the Commission conducts investigations, issues complaints, holds hearings, and enters cease-and-desist orders in cases of proved violations.

Provision is made for appeal to the circuit courts of appeals of the United States, which may affirm, modify, or set aside orders of the Commission. Provision is likewise made for orders to cease and desist issued by the Commission under authority of the Federal Trade Commission Act to become final within 60 days, unless previously appealed. Violation of the cease-and-desist orders issued under the Federal Trade Commission Act, after such orders have become final, subjects the violator to civil penalties in suits instituted by the Attorney General.

Investigations

Section 6 of the Federal Trade Commission Act empowers the Commission, whether on its own initiative or on the direction of the President or Congress, or on the application of the Attorney General, to investigate the organization, business, conduct, practices, and management of any corporation engaged in commerce, excepting banks and common carriers subject to the act to regulate commerce, and its relation to other corporations, to individuals, associations, and partnerships and to require by general or special orders, corporations engaged in commerce, excepting banks and common carriers, to file with the Commission in such form as the Commission may prescribe annual or special, or both annual and special, reports or answers in writing to specific questions, furnishing to the Commission such information as it may require as to the organization, business, conduct, practices, management, and relation to other corporations, partnerships, and individuals of the respective corporations filing such reports or answers in writing.

CLAYTON ACT

The Federal Trade Commission and the Department of Justice are invested with concurrent jurisdiction to restrain violations of the Clayton Act.

Price Discrimination

The Commission administers those provisions of the Robinson-Patman Act [of 1936] which amend the antidiscrimination inhibitions of section 2 of the Clayton Act. Discriminations in price not justified by savings in cost, nor otherwise justifiable under the act, are forbidden where the effect of such discrimination may be substantially to lessen competition.

Exclusive Dealing Arrangements

It is a function of the Commission, under section 3 of the Clayton Act, to prevent the lease or sale of commodities, or the fixing of a price, or discount from or rebate upon such price, on the condition, agreement, or understanding that the lessee or purchaser shall not use or deal in the commodities of a competitor where the effect of such lease or sale, or such conditions, agreement, or understanding may be substantially to lessen competition or tend to create a monopoly in any line of commerce.

Corporate Acquisitions

Section 7 of the Clayton Act as amended by the Celler-Kefauver Act (Dec. 29, 1950, Public Law 899, 64 Stat. 1125), charges the Commission with the prevention of unlawful corporate acquisitions. This section prohibits any corporation from acquiring the whole or any part of capital stock or other assets in any other corporation where the effect of such acquisition may be substantially to lessen competition or tend to create a monopoly of any line of commerce in any section of the country.

Interlocking Directorates

The Commission is charged with preventing unlawful directorates as defined in section 8 of the Clayton Act. This section prohibits any director from serving on the boards of two or more corporations then or theretofore in competition by virtue of business and location, so that elimination of competition by agreement would violate the antitrust laws, provided any one of the corporations has capital, surplus, and undivided profits aggregating more than $1 million. . . .

Index

About the Author

Dr. Mueller is Vilas Professor of Agricultural Economics and a professor in the department of economics and the law school at the University of Wisconsin. He was Executive Director of the President's Cabinet Committee on Price Stability from 1968 to 1969; Director of the Bureau of Economics, Federal Trade Commission, from 1961 to 1968; and Chief Economist of the House of Representatives' Small Business Committee in 1961. He taught at the University of California from 1954 to 1957 and the University of Wisconsin from 1957 to 1961, was Professorial Lecturer at American University from 1963 to 1964, a Visiting Professor at Michigan State University in the Fall of 1965 and on the staff of the University of Maryland from 1965 to 1969. He has contributed articles to many journals, including the *American Economic Review*, the *Review of Economics and Statistics*, the *Journal of Marketing*, and the *Southern Economic Review*. His book, *The Changing Structure of Food Retailing*, written in collaboration with Leon Garoian, was published in 1961.